The
JANE AUSTEN
Cookbook

The
JANE AUSTEN
Cookbook

Maggie Black & Deirdre Le Faye

CHICAGO
REVIEW
PRESS

Authors' Acknowledgments

I am most grateful to the Jane Austen Memorial Trust, for permission to study Martha Lloyd's MS volume, and for the use of her daguerreotype; and to Peter Stringer, for photographs of the daguerreotype and of the page from Martha's book.

D.L.F.

Every historical book owes an immeasurable debt to the past people and circumstances which gave it birth, so my primary debt is to Martha Lloyd, the Austen girls' close companion, and to the friends who gave Martha their recipes.

I owe a similar debt to many modern friends and colleagues. First to Ewart Wells who did much of the recipe testing, to Denise Abbott, Mary Norwak, Anne Nicholls, Nicola Hartopp of the Herb Society and Priscilla Bain who gave me recipes. Wendy Evans of the Museum of London, Silvija Davidson, Sri Owen, Mike Bull of the Wandsworth Museum, C. Anne Wilson of the Brotherton Library, Leeds, Joanna Booth, Philip and Mary Hyman and several others generously gave me access to their scholarship.

Products and good advice came from Sallie Morris on behalf of Cherry Valley Farms and from Guy Woodall who makes Thorncroft Cordials, from Donal Box, fishmonger, and Randalls, butchers. Keddies Ltd, makers of Geo. Watkins's traditional sauces and ketchups, and Carpenter's Putney Exchange, supplier of storage jars, also deserve recognition.

Writing my part of this book has been a great experience, but it could not have been brought to fruition without the kindly and patient care of the British Museum Press editors Nina Shandloff and Ruth Baldwin. Nor could it have been brought to life at all without the detailed and wise guidance and helpful goodwill of my fellow author Deirdre Le Faye.

M.K.B.

Recipes © 1995 Maggie Black
Introduction © 1995 Deirdre Le Faye

First published in Great Britain by British Museum Press
A division of British Museum Publications Ltd
46 Bloomsbury Street, London WC1B 3QQ

Published in the United States by Chicago Review Press, Inc.
814 N. Franklin Street, Chicago, Illinois, 60610

Designed by Behram Kapadia
Set in Postscript Baskerville
Printed in Great Britain by The Bath Press, Avon

ISBN 1-55652-242-8   LC #94-45293   641.5941 A933

1   2   3   4   5   6   7   8   9   10

Illustration Acknowledgments

The publishers would like to thank the following for supplying illustrations (numbers refer to page numbers): Trustees of the British Museum, London, 27; Jane Austen Memorial Trust, 34, 37; Metropolitan Museum of Art, New York, 9, 13; National Portrait Gallery, London, 7; Opie Collection of Children's Literature, Bodleian Library, Oxford, 58; Tate Gallery, London, 24.

CONTENTS

INTRODUCTION

This book contains a selection of recipes dating back to the late Georgian/Regency period, from approximately 1750 to 1820, modernised for present-day kitchens. These years also encompass Jane Austen's own brief lifespan (1775–1817), and the dishes chosen are those such as she and her family, and the characters in her novels, would have eaten. It is hoped, therefore, that the book will be of interest and practical use both to those cooks who enjoy recreating dishes of the past, and to Austenian enthusiasts who would like more information concerning the food and meals mentioned in Jane's novels and letters.

From the seventeenth to the early nineteenth century, before printed texts by professional cooks became freely available, most ladies compiled their own manuscript volume of domestic recipes.

The bill of fare in one house would not be so like that in another as it is now, for family receipts [the contemporary word] were held in high estimation. A grandmother of culinary talent could bequeath to her descendant fame for some particular dish, and might influence the family dinner for many generations.... One house would pride itself on its ham, another on its game-pie, and a third on its superior furmity, or tansey-pudding.

Some of the recipes in this book are taken from two volumes of just such a nature, whose owners were connected with the Austens; one belonged to Martha Lloyd (1765–1843), who lived with Mrs George Austen, Cassandra and Jane in Hampshire for a number of years, so we may be reasonably certain that her recipes were actually used in that household. The other was compiled by the diarist Mrs Philip Lybbe Powys (1738–1817) of Hardwick House, Oxfordshire, an old friend of Mrs George Austen and also connected by marriage, as her daughter Caroline married Mrs Austen's nephew, the Revd Edward Cooper; Mrs Powys's book has Austen family names attached to some recipes. Where these two domestic manuscripts do not give dishes mentioned by Jane in her writings, recipes have been drawn from contemporary published works. Anyone wishing to recreate an Austenian-style dinner party should therefore find sufficient recipes in this book with which to compose several complete menus.

Portrait of Jane Austen by her sister Cassandra.

Social and Domestic Life
in Jane Austen's time

'Invite him to dinner, Emma, and help him to the best of the fish and the chicken, but leave him to chuse his own wife.' This advice from Mr Knightley, at the end of Chapter I of *Emma*, sets the scene for all the subsequent misunderstandings and embarrassments that occur among Highbury society during the next twelve months, caused by Miss Wood-house's self-confident delight in matchmaking. But if we, the modern readers of Jane Austen's comedy of manners, were to find ourselves suddenly transported back in time to join in any of the dinner parties that follow – the Westons' at Randalls on Christmas Eve, the Coles' in February, or Emma's own at Hartfield in April – such a surprising journey would bring very forcibly to our attention the changes in social habits where mealtimes and food are concerned that have gradually taken place, almost unnoticed at the time, since the beginning of the nineteenth century.

To start with, the division of the day by mealtimes was in itself considerably different from our modern routine. We are now accustomed to the idea of having electricity instantly available to provide the artificial light that enables us to use as many hours out of the twenty-four as we wish in whatever form of occupation we choose, whether it be to breakfast early, dine late, read in bed or drive in safety on the roads at night. In the late eighteenth century, at the time of Jane Austen's birth, it was necessary to make the best possible use of the hours of daylight, since travelling after dark was always hazardous, even on a moonlit night; and candles, wood and coal were quite as expensive comparatively speaking as gas, oil and electricity and far more liable to be in short supply or to run out altogether during hard winters.

The rural labourers were, of course, even more dependent upon natural light for their work than were their employers, but the country squires and professional classes, such as Jane Austen describes in her novels, nevertheless also found it desirable to rise at about seven or eight and carry out a good deal of the day's business before sitting down to a solid breakfast at ten. This breakfast lasted about an hour, and thereafter the Georgian or Regency 'morning' extended right through the middle of the day until dinner at perhaps three or four o'clock in what we would now reckon to be the afternoon; during these 'morning' hours ladies

'The Reception' by Thomas Rowlandson (1756–1827).

would drive out to pay calls or go shopping, while the gentlemen continued to pursue the duties of their estate or profession. Dinner lasted about two hours; in summer a gentle stroll in the grounds or to some urban social promenade might follow, while in winter the family and guests would gather round the fire in the drawing-room for cards, conversation, perhaps impromptu music and dancing, until tea, accompanied by cakes or similar light refreshments, was served there at about eight o'clock. Depending on choice and circumstances, there might yet be a supper-tray brought in with wine and further cold food, about eleven o'clock or midnight.

This was the general pattern of the day as Jane Austen knew it, though the precise timing and content of meals would be qualified by a family's status and occupation and by the differences between the customs of town and country residents – London smart society usually dined at five o'clock or even later, and had their tea or light supper after returning from the theatre, whereas less fashionable middle-class families tended to have an earlier and smaller dinner, and finished the evening with a hot, cooked supper instead of the more elegant but less sustaining tea with cold snacks or nibbles. Guests could be invited either to join the family for dinner and stay on all the rest of the evening, or else to come later on just for the tea – as we might now say, to 'drop in for coffee afterwards'.

The prolonged and busy morning meant that there was no real need or accepted hour for lunch, and this meal crept only gradually into existence during the second half of the nineteenth century; by that time breakfasts had become earlier and dinners still later, so that lunch was viewed as a private family affair for mothers and children who needed some nourishment in the middle of the day, not yet as another social meal to which guests could be invited. Afternoon tea in the drawing-room, as we now know it – tea, with any combination of bread and butter, sandwiches, biscuits and sweet cakes, taken at about four or five o'clock – was the latest of modern meals to be created, a specifically social function invented by the leisured hostesses of the Edwardian era.

However, even if lunch did not officially exist in Jane Austen's lifetime, its origins were already there in the custom of offering refreshments to morning callers, who by definition would arrive between 11.00 am and 3.00 pm. Such refreshments could include cold meats, sandwiches, cake and seasonal or preserved fruits, which taken together could add up to quite a satisfying meal. If the morning's business were shopping in town rather than calling upon neighbours, pastry-cook shops would provide tarts, buns and other confectionery, to be washed down with a glass of whey, at a very modest charge. The coaching inns would also undertake to provide cold food for travellers breaking their journeys in between the recognised mealtimes. Such an unofficial small meal might be referred to, especially in the south of England, as a 'nuncheon' – a dialect word, with many variant spellings and pronounced something like 'noonshine'.

Having finished the morning's business, and spent perhaps an hour in dressing for dinner, the family would gather in the drawing-room to receive their guests; if the family included young children, these would be dressed in their best clothes and brought in to be introduced to the company for a few minutes, before being sent upstairs again to have their own simple supper in the nursery. The next differences that would surprise a time-travelling guest from the future would be the facts that no attempt was made to invite appropriate numbers of male and female friends to ensure their alternate placement at table, and that, indeed, there was no 'taking in' and no allotted placement. The host would certainly be the first to enter the dining-room, escorting the senior lady, but thereafter he took his accepted place at the foot of the table, facing the hostess, and left the senior lady to choose her own seat. The hostess sat at the upper end of the table, and it was understood that the places near her were the places of honour and so tacitly reserved for the senior guests. This haphazard arrangement did have its social benefit in that young gentlemen could manoeuvre to sit next to the young ladies of their choice – and perhaps, too, young ladies could manoeuvre themselves away from boring gentlemen and towards those upon whom they might have their own matrimonial intentions.

But the greatest difference between our dinners and those of Jane Austen's time originates from the change of meaning that has taken place in the deceptively simple word 'course', which has made a vast alteration in the actual quantity and presentation of the food. In a restaurant the phrase 'a two-course meal' now generally means a savoury (usually meat) dish followed by some form of sweet pudding or dessert; 'a three-course meal' implies that a plate of soup or other light starter precedes the savoury dish and the dessert; and we take it for granted that all the vegetables and sauces we deem proper to accompany such dishes will be served without further comment, and that the food, ready carved, sliced or apportioned, will be brought to us by waiters after we have sat down at the table and given our order. As far as our Georgian ancestors were concerned, as soon as they walked into the dining-room they saw before them a table already covered with separate dishes of every kind of food – soup, fish, meat, game, poultry, pies, vegetables, sauces, pickles, sweet and savoury puddings, custards and jellies – in number anything from five to twenty-five items, depending upon the grandeur of the occasion, and arranged symmetrically around the centre dish; this spread consti-tuted *a course* – and even then formed only part of the dinner.

When faced by this array of dishes, the host supervised the initial serving of soup (very often mulligatawny or turtle) and carved the large joints of meat (saddle of mutton, sirloin of beef, haunch of venison) that were brought in once the soup tureens had been removed. There was nearly always a salmon at one end of the table, balanced by a turbot surrounded by smelts at the other. After the host's carving, every gentleman helped himself from the dish in front of him and offered it to his neighbour, or else sent one of the attendant manservants to fetch another dish from a different part of the table. It was not expected that everybody should eat their way through everything, but that individuals should choose two or three of the items they preferred. Wine, beer, ale and soda water were served, again to cater for individual tastes. Some gentlemen preferred to drink port, sherry and hock with their food, on the grounds that claret and even burgundy were too thin and wishy-washy. After the soup had been served, it was customary for all, both ladies and gentlemen, to start 'taking wine' with each other – that is, drinking everybody's health round the table.

Once the guests had had as much as they required from the selection of foods first placed before them, an intermediate dessert of cheese, salad, raw celery and the like might be offered, and then the table was cleared and another equal quantity of different dishes – still including both savoury and sweet – was brought in to constitute the *second course*. After the guests had eaten themselves to a standstill on the second course, the table was cleared again and the cloth removed, to reveal either another cloth lying beneath or else the fine polished table, and the *dessert* was set out. This would include nuts and fruits, fresh or preserved depending upon the season, and perhaps sweetmeats and ice-creams, and was usually accompanied by port and Madeira, with sweet wine for the ladies. The nursery children, who had first been seen in the drawing-room before dinner commenced, were now brought in again, still dressed in their best clothes, to be given a small share in the dessert and to receive some tactful admiration and kisses from the guests, before finally being taken off to bed.

The company sat over dessert for about quarter of an hour, after which the ladies left the dining-room and settled themselves in the drawing-room. Here they would chat, embroider or flip through illustrated books for an hour or so, before ordering tea and coffee to be brought in, at which time the gentlemen would finish their drinking and discussions in the dining-room and join the ladies. Earlier in the Georgian era the masculine drinking group had usually preferred to linger together over their wine bottles for a very long time, but by the early nineteenth century it was quite permissible for individual gentlemen to move into the drawing-room whenever they wished. For the next couple of hours the company would occupy themselves as appropriate to the season and weather, until more tea, this time accompanied by light refreshments, was served in the drawing-room to complete the evening, unless a card party continued playing very late.

Such lavish entertaining was understandably a source of pride to the hostess, and equally a source of great interest to her guests and neighbours. Letters, memoirs and diaries of the period all frequently give

'The Squire's Kitchen' by Thomas Rowlandson.

descriptions of the meals that their writers enjoyed, and provide a fascinating insight into the standard of living of the middle and upper classes of Georgian society, such as Jane Austen would have known. In July 1779 Miss Catherine Hutton dined with the Revd Mr Shuttleworth, the rector of Aston in Derbyshire, and wrote to her father in Birmingham:

At three o'clock we sat down to table, which was covered with salmon at top, fennel sauce to it, melted butter, lemon pickle and soy; at the bottom a loin of veal roasted; on one side kidney beans, on the other peas, and in the middle a hot pigeon pie with yolks of eggs in. To the kidney beans and peas succeeded ham and chickens, and when everything was removed came a currant tart. Mr. Shuttleworth's behaviour was friendly and polite; he was attentive to the wants of his guests, and helped them to everything they wanted in a moment, without the least appearance of ceremony. He is sensible and lively, and I think the most of a gentleman of any man I ever knew. After dinner we had water to wash [that is, in finger-bowls], and when the cloth was taken away, gooseberries, currants and melon, wines and cyder. Mr. Shuttleworth asked me for a toast, and I gave him Mr. Rolleston, by whom we had been most elegantly entertained in that very room some years before. At a little before five, my mother, Sally Cocks, and I retired into the drawing room, where I amused myself with reading and looking at the prints till six, when I ordered tea, and sent to let the gentlemen know it was ready. Mr. Purcell and my uncle went away, Mr. Shuttleworth, Mr. Collier and Mr. Silver came and drank tea with us, which I made for them. After tea Mr. Shuttleworth and I chatted very sociably about Matlock, to which place he goes tomorrow. At seven o'clock we took leave, after having spent a most agreeable day.

Three days later Miss Hutton and her mother again dined out in a party of eight, and this time had 'three boiled chickens at top, a very fine haunch of venison at bottom; ham on one side, a flour pudding on the other, and beans in the middle. After the cloth was removed, we had gooseberries, and a remarkably fine dish of apricots. Miss Greaves and Miss Boothby worked at their netting and embroidery, while I was an idle spectator, as I had brought no work with me ...'

The diary of another bachelor country parson, the Revd James Woodforde of Weston Longeville in Norfolk, is now renowned for its copious details of the dinners at which he was either host or guest. Early in 1780 he dined with the squire's family, and for six people the dishes were

a Calf's Head, boiled Fowl and Tongue, a Saddle of Mutton rosted on the Side Table, and a fine Swan rosted with Currant Jelly Sauce for the first Course. The Second Course a couple of Wild Fowl called Dun Fowls, Larks, Blamange, Tarts, etc. etc. and a good Desert of Fruit after amongst which was a Damson Cheese. I never eat a bit of a Swan before, and I think it good eating with sweet sauce. The Swan was killed 3 weeks before it was eat and yet not the lest bad taste in it.

In June of the following year he entertained the squire with 'a Couple of Chicken boiled and a Tongue, a Leg of Mutton boiled and Capers and Batter Pudding for the first Course, Second, a couple of Ducks rosted and green Peas, some Artichokes, Tarts and Blancmange. After dinner, Almonds and Raisins, Oranges and Strawberries, Mountain and Port Wines. Peas and Strawberries the first gathered this year by me.'

Neither Mr Shuttleworth nor Mr Woodforde was particularly well off, hence their entertainments were not very large or elaborate by the standards of the time. Dinners for important guests obviously had to be much grander, and the Austen family's old friend Mrs Philip Lybbe Powys recorded proudly in her diary some of the dishes that she, as hostess for her bachelor brother-in-law the Dean of Canterbury, provided for Prince William of Gloucester, nephew of George III, when he visited Kent in the summer of 1798. On Saturday, 25 August, they sat down fourteen at table in all, and had before them:

	SALMON TROUT	
	SOLES	
FRICANDO OF VEAL		RAISED GIBLET PIE
	VEGETABLE PUDDING	
CHICKENS		HAM
	MUFFIN PUDDING	
CURRY OF RABBITS		PRESERVE OF OLIVES
SOUP		HAUNCH OF VENISON
OPEN TART SYLLABUB		RAISED JELLY
	THREE SWEETBREADS, LARDED	
MACCARONI		BUTTERED LOBSTER
	PEAS	
	POTATOES	
BASKETS OF PASTRY		CUSTARDS
	GOOSE	

In 1810–11, the years when *Sense and Sensibility* appeared and Jane Austen started revising *First Impressions* into *Pride and Prejudice*, Mr Louis Simond, a serious and intellectual Franco-American gentleman with an English wife, visited England for the first time and later published an account of his travels in and opinions of this country. Of the English dining habits he wrote:

There are commonly two courses and a dessert. I shall venture to give a sketch of a moderate dinner for ten or twelve persons –

First Course

OYSTER SAUCE	FOWLS	VEGETABLES
FISH	SOUP	ROASTED OR BOILED BEEF
SPINAGE	BACON	VEGETABLES

Second Course

CREAMS	PASTRY	CAULIFLOWERS
RAGOÛT À LA FRANÇAISE	CREAM	GAME
CELERY	MACARONI	PASTRY

Dessert

WALNUTS	CAKES	RAISINS AND ALMONDS
APPLES		PEARS
RAISINS AND ALMONDS		ORANGES

By the late 1820s signs of a slow change in dining customs were beginning to appear that would gradually convert the Georgian free-for-all across the table into the style we now recognise and consider appropriate to formal entertaining. After the final end, at Waterloo in 1815, of the decades of global warfare that had kept the English largely cooped up at home, foreign travel again became possible and rich tourists flocked across the Channel. Here they discovered that in Europe dinners were served 'à la Russe' – the food being cut up beforehand at the sideboard and the dishes then handed round by the servants – and consequently, when the 'most elegant of those who have been abroad' returned to England, they introduced this new and certainly much more convenient style of dining. Like all new fashions it took time to become established, but service à la Russe had become the norm at English dinner-parties by 1870 and is still with us today.

To be able to provide the ingredients for these vast meals was a never-ending problem for the hostess, involving continual culinary tasks and forward planning. Without modern methods of refrigeration, green-house cultivation and rapid air transport, in Jane Austen's time the staple items of diet were all home-produced, and so could be either fresher, staler or more pungent than their modern counterparts, depending upon local circumstances. For example, sea-fish by definition could be eaten thoroughly fresh only by those families who lived near the coast; it was transported inland for sale, but in warm weather might be barely fit to eat by the time it reached its ultimate destination, and at the very least would need a strongly flavoured sauce to make it palatable. Mary Russell Mitford (1787–1855), when writing her *Our Village* essays on country life in the South of England, described an itinerant chapman who travelled during the summer months with a noisy lumbering cart full of panniers through the counties of Hampshire, Berkshire and Oxfordshire, bring-ing with him from the Hampshire sea-coast crabs, shrimps, mussels, cockles, periwinkles, oysters, brill and herrings, and taking back nuts, apples and cherries.

Pork could be eaten fresh only during the colder half of the year, from approximately September to March, and once a pig had been killed most of the carcase had to be hurriedly pickled, salted or cured into ham and bacon, so that it could be kept in store and eaten during the warmer months. Beef and mutton were in season all the year round, and country squires could kill animals from their own farms as and when required; today we rarely eat mutton, but insist on having sheep killed young, as lamb. Rabbits, pigeons and wildfowl were available on common land to anyone who cared to shoot them, but game beasts and birds – venison, hare, grouse, partridge, pheasant – were the private property of the landowner, and as such were shot only by him and his family, or by friends with his permission. It was considered a great mark of consider-ation to present half a buck or a brace of birds to less wealthy neighbours who did not have their own game-preserves.

Nearly all housewives in the country kept their own poultry yard, which would yield the eggs and meat from turkeys, geese, ducks, chick-

ens, guinea-fowl and perhaps some hand-reared pheasants. A family might also have sufficient land to keep a house-cow, affording the fresh dairy products of milk, cream, butter, junket, cheese, buttermilk, and curds and whey. Bread, cakes, pies, puddings and pastries would all be home-baked. The walled kitchen garden produced a seasonal selection of green and root vegetables and soft fruit, while tree fruit – cherries, mulberries, apples, pears, plums, damsons, apricots, peaches, nectarines – and grape-vines would be grown within the shelter of the walls; beehives too would be placed in or near the orchards, to pollinate the flowers and provide honey later in the year. Keen gardeners like the Revd Gilbert White (1720–93), author of *The Natural History of Selborne*, a village not far from Jane Austen's last home at Chawton, constructed simple outdoor hot-beds and lovingly coddled melons and cucumbers to maturity despite the uncertain English weather; wealthier gentlemen were able to maintain proper heated greenhouses in which to grow the still-exotic pineapples, as well as enabling their melons, cucumbers, grapes and peaches to ripen more quickly and safely. Such delicate and expensive fruits were also valued as gifts, perhaps in exchange for the venison and game provided by those who preferred field-sports to gardening.

However, as all gardeners know, vegetables and fruit are available only for limited seasons and then usually produce in a short time larger quantities than can be immediately eaten by the gardener's family. Without the option of home freezing, in the past the careful housewife had to spend a large part of the summer months in salting, pickling, drying, potting, candying, jamming, cheese-making, brewing, wine-making, and generally storing and preserving in any other feasible way the various kinds of garden and dairy produce available to her. The 'usual offices' of a country kitchen might include an apple-room, pear-bin, cheese-loft and minced-meat closet, allocated and fitted up as particularly suitable for these individual stores. To neglect these summer tasks would mean going short during the following winter, when it would in all probability be difficult, if not impossible, to buy such foods.

For the town housewife, who could not command the space for her own dairy, poultry yard and vegetable garden, there was no option but to rely upon local shops or suppliers; this had the benefit of sometimes making food more rapidly available if suddenly required, but could also mean that it was less fresh and possibly even deliberately adulterated by the tradesman – watered milk and baker's bread made with bad flour were notorious in this respect. The luxury imported items such as tea, coffee, chocolate, sugar, rice, dried currants, oranges, lemons and spices always had to be purchased, either in small quantities from shops or in larger quantities direct from the importing merchant.

The difficulties of housekeeping on this scale, in order to produce dinners of the size and variety mentioned above, are vividly summarised by Mary Russell Mitford:

Every housewife can tell what a formidable guest is an epicure who comes to take pot-luck – how sure it is to be bad luck, especially when the unfortunate hostess lives five miles from a market town. Mr. Sidney always came unseasonably, on washing-day, or Saturday, or the day before a great party. So sure as we had a scrap dinner, so sure came he. My dear mother [used to] try all that could be done by potted meats and omelettes, and little things tossed up on a sudden to amend the bill of fare. But cookery is an obstinate art, and will have its time . . . the kickshaws [small made-up side-dishes] were half raw, the solids were mere rags; the vegetables were cold, the soup scalding; no shallots to the rump steaks; no mushrooms with the broiled chicken; no fish; no oysters; no ice; no pineapples. Poor Mr. Sidney! He must have had a great regard for us to put up with our bad dinners.

The Novels and the Letters

As Jane Austen placed her novels in contemporary settings, she had no need to spell out customs of the day with which her readers would already be fully conversant. She was much more interested in the social interaction of her characters than in what they ate, hence in her dinner-party scenes the emphasis is on their conversation and unspoken thoughts rather than on the food before them; indeed, it is significant that only her sillier or more unattractive characters talk specifically about food. While this authorial choice has deprived us of what would now be interesting period detail, we can nevertheless pick out from her works a number of references to food and mealtimes where they are given as background information to help define her characters.

As might be expected, these references are much more obvious in the deliberately farcical short stories of Jane's juvenilia than in the novels of her maturity; for example, in *Frederic and Elfrida* Charlotte and her aunt 'sat down to Supper on a young Leveret, a brace of Partridges, a leash of Pheasants & a Dozen of Pigeons', while in the *Memoirs of Mr Clifford* the hero was 'determined to comfort himself with a good hot Supper and therefore ordered a whole Egg to be boiled for him & his Servants'; the eponymous heroine of *The Beautifull Cassandra* 'proceeded to a Pastry-cooks where she devoured six ices, refused to pay for them, knocked down the Pastry Cook & walked away'; the elegant company in *The Visit* rejects the plebeian dishes of fried cowheel and onion, red herrings, tripe, liver and crow [pig's liver with the mesentery attached] and suet pudding; and in *A Fragment* the feeble invalid Melissa has a kind friend who persists in offering her toasted cheese, curry and the hashed remains of an old duck. In *Lesley Castle*, indeed, food is itself one of the central jokes, being the monomania of Miss Charlotte Lutterell's life, as we see from her letter to Miss Margaret Lesley:

Imagine how great the Dissapointment must be to me, when you consider that after having laboured both by Night and by Day, in order to get the Wedding dinner ready by the time appointed, after having roasted Beef, Broiled Mutton, and Stewed Soup enough to last the new-married Couple through the Honeymoon, I had the mortification of finding that I had been Roasting, Broiling and Stewing both the Meat and Myself to no purpose. Indeed my dear Freind, I never remember suffering any vexation equal to what I experienced on last Monday when my sister came running to me in the store-room with her face as White as a Whipt syllabub, and told me that Hervey had been thrown from his

Horse, had fractured his Scull and was pronounced by his surgeon to be in the most emminent Danger. 'Good God! (said I) you dont say so? Why what in the name of Heaven will become of all the Victuals! We shall never be able to eat it while it is good. However, we'll call in the Surgeon to help us. I shall be able to manage the Sir-loin myself, my Mother will eat the soup, and You and the Doctor must finish the rest.' Here I was interrupted, by seeing my poor Sister fall down to appearance Lifeless upon one of the Chests, where we keep our Table linen.... My Mother and I continued in the room with her, and when any intervals of tolerable Composure in Eloisa would allow us, we joined in heartfelt lamentations on the dreadful Waste in our provisions which this Event must occasion, and in concerting some plan for getting rid of them. We agreed that the best thing we could do was to begin eating them immediately, and accordingly we ordered up the cold Ham and Fowls, and instantly began our Devouring Plan on them with great Alacrity. We would have persuaded Eloisa to have taken a Wing of a Chicken, but she would not be persuaded. She was however much quieter than she had been; the convulsions she had before suffered having given way to an almost perfect Insensibility. We endeavoured to rouse her by every means in our power, but to no purpose. I talked to her of Henry. 'Dear Eloisa (said I) there's no occasion for your crying so much about such a trifle (for I was willing to make light of it in order to comfort her) I beg you would not mind it – You see it does not vex me in the least; though perhaps *I* may suffer most from it after all; for I shall not only be obliged to eat up all the Victuals I have dressed already, but must if Henry should recover (which however is not very likely) dress as much for you again; or should he die (as I suppose he will) I shall still have to prepare a Dinner for you whenever you marry any one else. So you see that tho' perhaps for the present it may afflict you to think of Henry's sufferings, Yet I dare say he'll die soon, and then his pain will be over and you will be easy, whereas my Trouble will last much longer for work as hard as I may, I am certain that the pantry cannot be cleared in less than a fortnight.'

Lesley Castle was written probably in 1792; by 1797, when Jane was working on *Sense and Sensibility*, she mentions food only where the references help either to delineate a character or to advance the plot. The mean-minded city-bred Fanny Dashwood persuades her husband that all he need do to support his stepmother and half-sisters is to send them 'presents of fish and game, and so forth, whenever they are in season'; whereas the elder Mrs Dashwood and her daughters have no sooner arrived at Barton Cottage in Devonshire than her cousin Sir John Middleton sends them 'a large basket full of garden stuff and fruit ... followed before the end of the day by a present of game.' At Barton Park Sir John delighted in organising large dinner-parties full of noisy young people (to which Jane Austen very wisely does not invite her readers), and 'in summer he was for ever forming parties to eat cold ham and chicken out of doors'; Lady Middleton's contribution to family life was to pet her howling children with bribes of sugarplums and apricot marmalade. In this respect Lady Middleton is very much her mother's daughter, for

when Mrs Jennings took Elinor and Marianne Dashwood to London with her, she 'was solicitous on every occasion for their ease and enjoyment, and only disturbed that she could not make them choose their own dinners at the inn, nor extort a confession of their preferring salmon to cod, or boiled fowls to veal cutlets'; and when Marianne receives Willoughby's letter of repudiation while she is staying in London, Mrs Jennings tries to comfort her with sweetmeats, olives, dried cherries and a glass of Constantia wine. It is also Mrs Jennings who points out to Elinor the desirability of Colonel Brandon's home, from a wife's point of view:

'Delaford is a nice place, I can tell you; exactly what I call a nice old fashioned place, full of comforts and conveniences; quite shut in with great garden walls that are covered with the best fruit-trees in the country; and such a mulberry tree in one corner! . . . . Then, there is a dove-cote, some delightful stewponds, and a very pretty canal . . . . A butcher hard by in the village, and the parsonage-house within a stone's throw. To my fancy, a thousand times prettier than Barton Park, where they are forced to send three miles for their meat, and have not a neighbour nearer than your mother.'

In *Pride and Prejudice* Mrs Bennet's 'poor nerves' luckily do not encourage her to worry about diets or cherish food fads; on the contrary, she is proud of keeping a 'very good table' and quick to boast to Bingley that 'we dine with four and twenty families'. The Bennets' dinnertime is four o'clock, but when Elizabeth visits the ailing Jane at Netherfield, she finds that, under the influence of Mrs Hurst, their summons to dinner comes at the much smarter and later hour of half-past six; 'and as for Mr. Hurst, by whom Elizabeth sat, he was an indolent man, who lived only to eat, drink, and play at cards, who when he found her prefer a plain dish to a ragout, had nothing to say to her'. Upon Mr Collins's first visit to Longbourn, 'the dinner too in its turn was highly admired; and he begged to know to which of his fair cousins, the excellence of its cookery was owing. But here he was set right by Mrs. Bennet, who assured him with some asperity that they were very well able to keep a good cook, and that her daughters had nothing to do in the kitchen.' At Rosings, Elizabeth finds that

the dinner was exceedingly handsome, and there were all the servants, and all the articles of plate which Mr. Collins had promised; and, as he had likewise foretold, he took his seat at the bottom of the table, by her ladyship's desire, and looked as if he felt that life could furnish nothing greater. – He carved, and ate, and praised with delighted alacrity; and every dish was commended, first by him, and then by Sir William, who was now enough recovered to echo whatever his son in law said, in a manner which Elizabeth wondered Lady Catherine could bear. But Lady Catherine seemed gratified by their excessive admiration, and gave most gracious smiles, especially when any dish on the table proved a novelty to them.

On her return from Kent, Elizabeth picks up Jane from the Gardiners' in London and the sisters arrive together about noon at the coaching inn in Meryton, where Kitty and Lydia have come to meet them; here they have what Lydia calls 'the nicest cold luncheon in the world', consisting of cold meat, salad and cucumber, before driving home to Longbourn for a large family dinner. Later in the summer, when Elizabeth makes her first morning visit to Pemberley, Miss Darcy's guests are offered 'cold meat, cake, and a variety of all the finest fruits in season', these latter being 'beautiful pyramids of grapes, nectarines, and peaches'. Mr Darcy invites Elizabeth and the Gardiners to dinner for the following day, but the party has to be cancelled as a result of the news of Lydia's elopement and we do not know what choice dishes the Pemberley estate might have provided for this occasion. We do hear Mrs Bennet's self-congratulations after a dinner for fifteen at Longbourn in September:

'I think every thing has passed off uncommonly well, I assure you. The dinner was as well dressed as any I ever saw. The venison was roasted to a turn – and every body said, they never saw so fat a haunch. The soup was fifty times better than what we had at the Lucas's last week; and even Mr. Darcy acknowledged, that the partridges were remarkably well done; and I suppose he has two or three French cooks at least.'

Mansfield Park and *Emma* are the two novels of Jane Austen's maturity that contain the most numerous references to food. When the ten-year-old Fanny Price first arrives at Mansfield, tired and homesick, a gooseberry tart cannot comfort her; and in later years we learn that the 'solemn procession, headed by Baddely [the butler], of tea-board, urn, and cake-bearers' saves her one evening from Henry Crawford's unwelcome

A banqueting table laid with pyramids of sweetmeats, from *The Court and Country Cook* (1702) by F. Massialot.

wooing, and that she much prefers to receive from Edmund's hands a glass of Madeira from the supper-tray. Once the miserly Mrs Norris has become a widow and left Mansfield parsonage, she directs her envious gaze upon her successors there, the Revd Dr and Mrs Grant:

The Grants showing a disposition to be friendly and sociable, gave great satisfaction in the main among their new acquaintance. They had their faults, and Mrs. Norris soon found them out. The Dr. was very fond of eating, and would have a good dinner every day; and Mrs. Grant, instead of contriving to gratify him at little expense, gave her cook as high wages as they did at Mansfield Park, and was scarcely ever seen in her offices. Mrs. Norris could not speak with any temper of such grievances, nor of the quantity of butter and eggs that were regularly consumed in the house. 'Nobody loved plenty and hospitality more than herself – nobody more hated pitiful doings – the parsonage she believed had never been wanting in comforts of any sort, had never borne a bad character in *her time*, but this was a way of going on that she could not understand. A fine lady in a country parsonage was quite out of place. *Her* store-room she thought might have been good enough for Mrs. Grant to go into. Enquire where she would, she could not find out that Mrs. Grant had ever had more than five thousand pounds.'

Mrs Grant soon stocks her poultry yard and plants her garden, and the apricot sapling which Sir Thomas Bertram had previously purchased for the parsonage, at a cost of seven shillings, becomes a bone of contention between Dr Grant and Mrs Norris as to whether it is or is not a Moor Park tree that can provide good-quality, fresh fruit for dessert, or whether its produce is suitable only for cooking. When Mrs Grant's younger brother and sister, Henry and Mary Crawford, come to stay with her, Henry's presence gives Dr Grant an excuse for drinking claret every day; on one occasion the Crawfords call rather unexpectedly late at Mansfield Park, and Mary explains that this visit has been due to her brother-in-law's bad temper – in her opinion he is

'an indolent selfish bon vivant, who must have his palate consulted in every thing, who will not stir a finger for the convenience of any one, and who, moreover, if the cook makes a blunder, is out of humour with his excellent wife. To own the truth, Henry and I were partly driven out this very evening, by a disappointment about a green goose, which he could not get the better of. My poor sister was forced to stay and bear it.'

Mary also reports another domestic contretemps a few days later: '"Dr. Grant is ill," said she, with mock solemnity. "He has been ill ever since he did not eat any of the pheasant today. He fancied it tough – sent away his plate – and has been suffering ever since."'

The Grants seem to be particularly unlucky with their poultry dishes, for Mrs Grant's invitation at short notice to Edmund and Fanny to dine at the parsonage is partly due to the fact that, as she says,

'Plucking the Turkey' by Henry Walton (1746–1813).

'... cook has just been telling me that the turkey, which I particularly wished not to be dressed till Sunday, because I know how much more Dr. Grant would enjoy it on Sunday after the fatigues of the day, will not keep beyond to-morrow. These are something like grievances, and make me think the weather most unseasonably close.'

'The sweets of housekeeping in a country village!' said Miss Crawford archly. 'Commend me to the nurseryman and the poulterer.'

'My dear child, commend Dr. Grant to the deanery of Westminster or St. Paul's, and I should be as glad of your nurseryman and poulterer as you could be. But we have no such people in Mansfield ... there is no escaping these little vexations, Mary, live where we may; and when you are settled in town and I come to see you, I dare say I shall find you with yours, in spite of the nurseryman and the poulterer – or perhaps on their very account. Their remoteness and unpunctuality, or their exorbitant charges and frauds will be drawing forth bitter lamentations.'

Mrs Norris's resentment at this invitation to Fanny leads to her tirade:

'And I hope you will have a very *agreeable* day and find it all mighty *delightful*. But I must observe, that five is the very awkwardest of all possible numbers to sit down to table; and I cannot but be surprized that such an *elegant* lady as Mrs. Grant should not contrive better! And round their enormous great wide table too, which fills up the room so dreadfully! Had the Doctor been contented to take my dining table when I came away, as any body in their senses would have done, instead of having that absurd new one of his own, which is wider, literally wider than the dinner table here – how infinitely better it would have been! ... Five, only five to be sitting round that table! However, you will have dinner enough on it for ten I dare say.'

When Sir Thomas returns from his trip to Antigua, and all the Bertram family dines at the Parsonage,

...the dinner itself was elegant and plentiful, according to the usual style of the Grants, and too much according to the usual habits of all to raise any emotion except in Mrs. Norris, who could never behold either the wide table or the number of dishes on it with patience, and who did always contrive to experience some evil from the passing of the servants behind her chair, and to bring away some fresh conviction of its being impossible among so many dishes but that some must be cold.

The last news Jane Austen gives about the Grants, after the calamity of Henry Crawford's elopement with Maria Rushworth, is that the Doctor obtained a stall at Westminster, which afforded a tactful excuse for leaving Mansfield in favour of residence in London, and that he thereafter 'brought on apoplexy and death, by three great institutionary dinners in one week'.

As for the Bertram family's entertaining, in the absence of both Sir Thomas, abroad, and Tom, gone off to Newmarket races, Mary Crawford thought that she would particularly notice the absence of the latter;

...and on their all dining together at the Park soon after his going, she retook her chosen place near the bottom of the table, fully expecting to feel a most melancholy difference in the change of masters. It would be a very flat business, she was sure. In comparison with his brother, Edmund would have nothing to say. The soup would be sent round in a most spiritless manner, wine drank without any smiles, or agreeable trifling, and the venison cut up without supplying one pleasant anecdote of any former haunch, or a single entertaining story about 'my friend such a one'.

On this occasion, however, Mr Rushworth, now engaged to Maria, was also present, boring the company with his incoherent plans for improvements at Sotherton, and 'Edmund was glad to put an end to his speech by a proposal of wine.' The Bertram dinner-table is of course equipped with 'silver forks, napkins, and finger glasses'.

The raucous and impoverished Price household in Portsmouth comes as a great shock to Fanny when she returns there after eight years at Mansfield Park. There is no butcher in the street where the Prices live, so Mrs Price claims that it is difficult to find time to 'dress a steak'. Fanny's three youngest brothers demand toasted cheese for supper after school, and her father shouts to the sluttish maidservant Rebecca for his rum and water. The bread and butter is greasy, the milk watered and bluish, and Fanny is 'so little equal to Rebecca's puddings, and Rebecca's hashes, brought to table as they all were, with such accompaniments of half-cleaned plates, and not half-cleaned knives and forks, that she was very often constrained to defer her heartiest meal, till she could send her brothers in the evening for biscuits and buns.'

In *Emma* the valetudinarian Mr Woodhouse, aged before his time, is always to be found fussing about health and diet. 'His own stomach could bear nothing rich, and he could never believe other people to be different from himself.' When the old ladies of Highbury come to play cards with him in the evenings, he offers them cooked suppers rather than just a tea-tray – 'He loved to have the cloth laid, because it had been the fashion of his youth; but his conviction of suppers being very unwholesome made him rather sorry to see any thing put on it.' In the course of the story we learn that some of these supper dishes are soft-boiled eggs, minced chicken and scalloped oysters, followed by apple tart and custard (but *no* 'unwholesome preserves'), also a fricassee of sweetbreads with asparagus, followed by tea, biscuits, cake, muffins, baked apples and wine. Oddly enough Mr Woodhouse is prepared to eat fried pork steaks 'without the smallest grease', but thinks roast pork quite indigestible. Emma sends a whole hind-quarter of one of their Hartfield porkers to Mrs and Miss Bates – 'There will be the leg to be salted ... and the loin to be dressed directly in any manner they like' – and her father agrees '... that if the leg is not over-salted, and then thoroughly boiled and eaten very moderately of, with a boiled turnip, and a little carrot or parsnip, I do not consider it unwholesome.'

The larger Highbury world contains Mr Knightley's Donwell Abbey estate, and every year he sends a sack of his cooking-apple crop to the impoverished Bates family; one of his tenants is Robert Martin of Abbey Mill Farm, whom Harriet Smith eventually marries. The main street of Highbury contains several shops, the most important of which is Mrs Ford's drapery, and others close by include a butcher and Mr Wallis's bakery with a little bow-window displaying gingerbread. Miss Bates buys her bread here, and also gets Mr Wallis to bake the apples provided by Mr Knightley – Mr Woodhouse thinks apples should be thrice-baked, but the Bateses believe that twice is quite sufficient – and these baked apples are then kept in Miss Bates's closet to be offered to morning callers, together with sweet cake from the beaufet. The vulgar Mrs Elton, upon her arrival as a bride, claims to be 'a little shocked at the want of two drawing rooms, at the poor attempt at rout-cakes, and there being no ice in the Highbury card parties', but the Revd Mr Elton is happy to accept a recipe for brewing homely spruce beer from Mr Knightley.

Mr Elton, who turns out to be as vulgar and conceited as his wife, unfortunately does *not* woo little Harriet Smith and so defeats Emma's matchmaking plans; in the lane Emma overtakes them deep in conversation, but 'experienced some disappointment when she found that he was only giving his fair companion an account of the yesterday's party at his friend Cole's, and that she was come in herself for the Stilton cheese, the north Wiltshire, the butter, the cellery, the beet-root and all the dessert'. At the Coles' next dinner-party, in February, Frank Churchill

chooses to sit beside Emma; on this occasion none of the food is mentioned, but Emma and Frank gossip and flirt together under cover of the general noise, and only have to be 'as formal and as orderly as the others' when conversation is interrupted by 'the awkwardness of a rather long interval between the courses ... but when the table was again safely covered, when every corner dish was placed exactly right, and occupation and ease were generally restored', Emma was able to resume her naughty speculations about Jane Fairfax and the Dixons.

A butcher's shop in Bishopsgate, London, by George Scharf (1788–1860).

As well as pork, there is mention of roast mutton and rice pudding at Hartfield on Christmas Eve for Mr John Knightley's little boys, and at the Randalls dinner-party that same evening a saddle of mutton seems to be the most important dish. For the strawberry party at Donwell Abbey the following summer, Mr Knightley provides an early dinner of cold meats in the house, with spruce beer and Madeira-and-water to quench late-June thirsts; pigeon pies and cold lamb are mentioned in connection with the Box Hill picnic. The supper table for the ball at the Crown causes Miss Bates to squeak with delight: 'Dear Jane, how shall we ever recollect half the dishes for grandmamma? Soup too!' – but on this occasion Jane Austen does not choose to specify the precise components of the spread that good Mrs Stokes had prepared. However, from references to other balls in the novels, it is clear that the fare was more or less standard: there was always white soup, cold ham, turkey, chicken and other cold meats, and creams and jellies, with negus to drink. Mrs Norris is careful to collect the jellies left over from the Mansfield Park ball and take them home with her, ostensibly for the benefit of her sick maidservant.

The Morlands in their parsonage at Fullerton have too large a family to be able to indulge in luxuries, hence when Catherine visits Northanger Abbey she is amazed at the variety of General Tilney's breakfast table, including the cocoa he drinks while reading his newspaper, and the fine, white 'French' bread which Mrs Morland cannot afford. The General boasts with mock-modesty of his Staffordshire breakfast service – 'quite an old set, purchased two years ago' – and is delighted to escort Catherine round his enormous kitchen-garden. 'The walls seemed countless in number, endless in length; a village of hot-houses seemed to arise among them, and a whole parish to be at work within the inclosure.' Continuing his inverse boasting, the General laments that with all his care he has been able to grow only a hundred pineapples the previous year. There is a 'tea-house' [summer-house] elsewhere in the Abbey grounds, and the General prides himself on donating twice a year half a buck from his parkland herd to the local gentlemen's club. The Abbey dinner is served on the dot of five o'clock, and when the Tilneys visit Henry's parsonage at Woodston it is a concession on his father's part that dinner there is served at four o'clock, to allow for driving home before dark. Here again, the General is quick to point out to Catherine that the parsonage 'has an excellent kitchen-garden ... the walls surrounding which I built and stocked myself about ten years ago, for the benefit of my son'.

Heated glasshouses, like these drawn by Humphry Repton in 1816, supplied the gentry with exotic fruits.

In the fragmentary *The Watsons* Jane Austen created a clerical family far poorer than the Morlands, to the extent that Elizabeth Watson had to say to her guests, 'You see your dinner' (meaning that the one course already on the table was all that she could offer them); and when Elizabeth and her young sister Emma dined alone together, it seems that they had only the one dish of 'fried beef'. The Watsons dined at three o'clock and had supper at nine, whereas the unfriendly Lord Osborne and his family at Osborne Castle did not start dinner till eight and finished at midnight.

There are hardly any specific references to food in *Persuasion*, which is not surprising, as the narrative is the most introspective and private of all the six novels. Hospitality – or the lack of it – symbolises the difference between life at Uppercross and at Bath; at the former, the Musgroves 'were visited by every body, and had more dinner parties, and more callers, more visitors by invitation and by chance, than any other family'. When Anne Elliot and Lady Russell called at Uppercross in the Christmas holidays, the drawing-room presented 'a fine family-piece' – 'on one side was a table, occupied by some chattering girls, cutting up silk and gold paper; and on the other were tressels and trays, bending under the weight of brawn and cold pies, where riotous boys were holding high revel; the whole completed by a roaring Christmas fire, which seemed determined to be heard, in spite of all the noise of the others'. By contrast Sir Walter Elliot's evening amusements in Bath 'were solely in the elegant stupidity of private parties', with Elizabeth Elliot taking her cue from a certain Lady Alicia who did not even ask her own sister's family to dinner, though they were in Bath for a month. Ironically the casual superficiality of city life nevertheless could lead to something deeper – thanks to the proximity of Mrs Molland's pastry-cook shop at No. 2 Milsom Street when rain made the elegant company seek refuge, Captain Wentworth and Anne found themselves sheltering there together and he noticed for the first time the attention being paid to her by Mr William Elliot, which led to the reawakening of his own old affection for her.

All these fictional meals and manners are clear reflections of the facts of Jane Austen's own life and the social circles in which she moved. During her childhood and early adult life at Steventon in Hampshire, when she was one of a large family group, her father's glebe farm provided them with fresh pork and mutton; her mother kept a poultry yard and little dairy herd, and managed the sunny kitchen garden on the south side of the house, where there were strawberry beds, cucumber frames, fruit trees and bushes (including Mrs Austen's favourite gooseberries) and a grape vine, as well as potatoes, then almost unknown as a domestic crop. 'They were novelties to a tenant's wife who was entertained at Steventon Parsonage . . . and when Mrs Austen advised her to

Steventon Parsonage,
Hampshire, home of Jane
Austen during her childhood
and early adult life.

plant them in her own garden, she replied, "No, no; they are very well for
you gentry, but they must be terribly *costly to rear*."' Cassandra, as she
grew up, was apparently responsible for keeping bees, which would
provide wax, honey and home-brewed mead; white wine is also mentioned as a family drink, but not red. In the later Steventon years,
between 1796 and 1801, Jane's letters to Cassandra mention a few of the
plain but healthy dishes eaten by the family at their 3.30 pm dinner –
boiled chicken, ragout veal, haricot mutton, fresh pork (Mrs Austen was
apparently especially fond of the spare-ribs), ox-cheek with little dumplings, pea soup and cold souse [lightly pickled pork brawn].

Jane and her parents visited Bath in the 1790s and also lived there,
when Mr Austen retired, from 1801 until after his death in 1805. During
these years of city life her letters refer now and then to the cost of basic
foodstuffs, the purchase of tea, coffee and sugar, and the availability of
such imported luxuries as almonds, raisins, French plums and tamarinds
[an East Indian fruit] in the Bath grocers' shops; and of course to the
local speciality, Bath buns. As part of the social life of the city, 'public
breakfasts' were held in the Sydney Gardens every morning, during the
season.

In 1806 the widowed Mrs Austen and her daughters went to live in
Southampton, in a large rented house in Castle Square, and for a time
shared these lodgings with Captain Francis (Frank) Austen and his young
wife Mary Gibson. The household also included Martha Lloyd (sister of
James Austen's second wife), who was without a permanent home of her
own following her old mother's death in 1805. Martha had already
compiled a manuscript book of culinary and other domestic recipes, and
no doubt her favourite dishes formed part of the Austens' daily fare. The

family now dined at five o'clock and their visitors often included Frank's naval friends; again, Jane's letters to Cassandra mention some of the particular items eaten – rice pudding, apple dumplings, apple pie, boiled leg of mutton (on one occasion this was unfortunately very much under-done), partridges, pheasants and a hare. Their friends the Fowle family of Kintbury, Berkshire, sent hampers of apples and a basket with poultry, and this latter Jane returned to them packed with four pairs of small soles, which had cost her six shillings. Mrs Austen hastened to plant currants, raspberries and gooseberries in their new garden, and the family made their own orange wine and also Martha's favourite spruce beer. On one December day they gave a small evening party, lasting from 7.00 until 11.30 pm, and the supper-tray included widgeon [a species of wild duck, so this was presumably served as a pâté], preserved ginger, and black butter [a sweetmeat with a basis of apple pulp]. When Frank and his Mary had had their first baby, and felt in need of a home of their own, they moved to the Isle of Wight, and for a parting gift, as Jane wrote: 'My mother has undertaken to cure six Hams for Frank; – at first it was a distress, but now it is a pleasure'; and this, or something like it, was the recipe she used:

The Revd George and Mrs Austen, Jane's parents.

Take two legs of Pork, each leg weighing about 15 pounds, rub them well over with two oz. of Saltpetre finely beaten, let them lie a day and night then take two pound of Brown Sugar, one pound & half of common Salt, mix them together and rub your Hams with it, let them lie three Weeks turn and rub them in the pickle every day.

From 1809 until her death in 1817 Jane Austen's home was at Chawton Cottage; the household now consisted of only Mrs Austen and her daughters and Martha Lloyd, and their combined income was modest, but they kept a warm welcome for all other members of the family and frequently had several of Mrs Austen's grandchildren staying for long periods. Mrs Austen was beginning to feel her age (in 1809 she was seventy) and did not set up a domestic dairy herd again, but she returned to keeping poultry and growing her own vegetables, as she had done at Steventon in earlier years. The Cottage's garden was planted with fruit trees – Orleans plums, greengages, apricots and mulberries are men-tioned – and also with potatoes, peas, strawberries, currants (these were to be made into wine) and gooseberries; in July 1814 Mrs Austen wrote charmingly to her granddaughter Anna: 'We have ... a very good crop of small Fruit, even your Gooseberry Tree does better than heretofore, when the Gooseberries are ripe I shall sit upon my Bench, eat them & think of you, tho' I can do that without the assistance of ripe gooseberries; indeed, my dear Anna, there is nobody I think of oftener, very few I love better.' Cassandra also presumably returned to bee-keeping, as the making of mead is referred to several times in Jane's letters of these years.

Orange wine was still a family favourite, for in one of Jane's last letters, not long before her death, she asked her friend Alethea Bigg for a recipe to use Seville oranges for this purpose. The family meals included beef pudding, neck of mutton, duck and green peas, and apple pies, with half a Stilton cheese sent from London by Henry Austen. Martha's sister Mary, whose husband James Austen had become rector of Steventon in succession to his father, on various occasions sent to her mother-in-law fresh pork, ham, sea-kale and pickled cucumbers.

This small group of single women, living quietly, did not pretend to keep fashionable hours, and Jane Austen's day at this period of her life seems to have had almost a modern pattern to it; according to her niece Caroline Austen's memories, Jane was in charge of the stores of tea, sugar and wine, and prepared breakfast for the family at nine o'clock. 'Luncheon' and 'dinner' then formed the other divisions of the day – so presumably the Austens took their meals at times convenient to themselves rather than sticking rigidly to social custom. On one occasion the rector of Chawton, the Revd Mr Papillon, invited Jane to his dinner-party, and in telling Cassandra about it afterwards Jane mentioned that the fare included mutton, mince pies, jellies, almonds and raisins, but no stewed pears. Mr Papillon was a bachelor, and Jane amusedly noted the efforts of two spinster ladies to attract his attention:

I could see nothing very promising between Mr. P. and Miss P.T. [Patty Terry]. She placed herself on one side of him at first, but Miss Benn obliged her to move up higher; & she had an empty plate, & even asked him to give her some Mutton twice without being attended to for some time. There might be design in this, to be sure, on his side; he might think an empty Stomach the most favourable for Love.

While her own lifestyle in Hampshire remained fairly modest and homely, Jane Austen was often able to enjoy the 'Elegance & Ease & Luxury' of wealthier circles, when she visited her brother Edward and his in-laws in Kent, or her brother Henry in London. Edward had been adopted by a distant cousin, Mr Thomas Knight, who owned the three estates of Steventon and Chawton in Hampshire and Godmersham Park in Kent, at which latter place Edward subsequently lived and brought up his large family. Mr Knight's widow retired to Canterbury, not far away, and the Bridges family, to which Edward's wife Elizabeth belonged, was at Goodnestone, close to Godmersham; so that constant visiting and entertaining took place among all these relations and their connections. With such dinners in mind, Jane gleefully assured Cassandra: 'I shall eat Ice & drink French wine, & be above vulgar Economy.' Edward always drank coffee for breakfast, and claret, port and Madeira at his dinners, and his estates could provide venison and all manner of game; Jane also mentions eating goose, and tomatoes ('tomatas', as she spells them), which at that date were still a rare and unfamiliar crop, and correspondingly expensive. These Kentish gentry kept more fashionable hours – dinners were at five o'clock or even later, finishing perhaps at eight o'clock; Jane referred to the Godmersham evening as being 'short', because it did not start till 10.00 pm and even then was broken by supper. On one occasion, when she stayed with Mrs Knight in Canterbury, after the other dinner guests had departed Jane and her hostess had an informal private supper together of 'tart and jelly' in Mrs Knight's dressing-room at ten o'clock.

For a number of years Jane's fourth brother, Henry, was a banker and army agent and lived in London; Mrs Austen used to send up turkeys and mead from Hampshire, and Edward and other friends provided him with game and fruit from their estates. When Jane visited Henry, she quite often started her shopping trips even before the ten o'clock breakfast time, in order to get served quickly ahead of the mid-morning crowds; she then dined at five o'clock – for example, on soup, fish, bouillée [boiled or stewed meat], partridges and apple tart – before going to the theatre at seven, and had more soup, with wine and water to drink, upon returning home at half-past eleven. One of Henry's favourite dishes seems to have been a 'boiled loaf' [a form of very light bread pudding], which was served apparently with raspberry jam.

On her mother's side of the family, Jane's rich Leigh cousins lived at Stoneleigh Abbey, near Kenilworth in Warwickshire; in the summer of 1806 the Austens stayed there for some days, and Mrs Austen's letter to her daughter-in-law Mary Lloyd gives a complete picture of the domestic economy of a prosperous Georgian estate:

... at nine in the morning we meet and say our prayers in a handsome Chapel ... then follows Breakfast, consisting of Chocolate Coffee & Tea – Plumb Cake, Pound Cake, Hot Rolls, Cold Rolls, Bread & Butter and dry toast for me – The House-Steward (a fine large respectable looking Man) orders all these matters ... We walk a great deal, for the Woods are impenetrable to the sun even in the middle of an August day – I do not fail to spend some time every day in the Kitchen Garden, where the quantities of small fruits exceed any thing you can form an idea of; this large family, with the assistance of a great many Blackbirds & Thrushes cannot prevent its rotting on the Trees – the Garden contains 5 acres and a half – The ponds supply excellent Fish, the Park excellent Venison – There is also great plenty of Pigeons Rabbits and all sort of Poultry – a delightful Dairy, where is made Butter, good Warwickshire Cheese and Cream Ditto – One Man Servant is called the Baker, he does nothing but Brew & Bake – The quantity of Casks in the Strong Beer Cellar is beyond imagination – those in the small Beer Cellar bears no proportion, tho' by the bye the small Beer may be called Ale without a misnomer ...

Martha Lloyd and her Recipe Book

Martha Lloyd in old age.

Martha Lloyd (1765–1843) was the eldest daughter of the Revd Nowes Lloyd, rector of Enborne, near Newbury, Berkshire, and his wife Martha Craven; her second sister Eliza (1768–1839) married in 1788 a cousin, the Revd Fulwar-Craven Fowle, and lived at Kintbury in Berkshire; and her youngest sister Mary (1771–1843) married the Revd James Austen, as his second wife, and lived at Deane and Steventon in Hampshire before moving to Speen in Berkshire when she became a widow. After Mr Lloyd's death in 1789 his widow and her two unmarried daughters rented Deane parsonage from the Revd George Austen for some years, before moving a few miles north to Ibthorpe, a hamlet in Upper Hurstbourne, Hampshire. In 1796 Martha was in love with a certain 'Mr. W.', but this romance came to nothing, and following Mary's marriage to James Austen in 1797 she lived alone with her mother until Mrs Lloyd's death in 1805, after which Martha joined forces with Mrs George Austen, Cassandra and Jane, and moved with them to Chawton Cottage. She stayed at Chawton until 1828, when she became the second wife of Captain Francis Austen, and lived with him and his younger children at Portsdown Lodge, near Portsmouth, until her death in 1843.

Like many ladies of her time, Martha made a collection of culinary and household recipes; hers is in a quarto notebook, bound in white vellum and originally containing 126 pages, watermarked but not dated. She signed her name on the inside back cover, but unfortunately did not give any indication as to when she started using the notebook; probably it was while she was living at Ibthorpe and no doubt gradually taking over more of the domestic responsibilities from the elderly Mrs Lloyd. The white vellum binding is now yellow-brown with age and wear, several of the pages are missing and others, especially those at the beginning of the book, are loose, frayed and heavily stained. Some of the entries are very faded, and on other pages the ink is so thick and black that it shows through to confuse the writing on the other side. From the front of the book, working forward to page 98, culinary recipes were entered; the book was then reversed, and some pages set aside to provide space for an index to these entries. Following the index, household recipes occupy twenty-four unnumbered pages, until they meet the culinary recipes on page 99 proper; these household recipes are unindexed. In some cases Martha gives the name of the person from whom she received the recipe, and in a few other cases the donor herself wrote the entry. The book accompanied Martha to her new home at Portsdown Lodge, and descended to one of the great-granddaughters of Admiral Sir Francis Austen (as he eventually became), who sold it to the Jane Austen Memorial Trust about thirty years ago. It is now usually on display at Jane Austen's house in Chawton.

The book contains 141 culinary recipes, but this total includes some which oddly enough are word-for-word repeats (was Martha very busy, or absent-minded?), so that the actual number of individual recipes is 135; the household recipes likewise total 53 with some repeated, the actual number being 49. The culinary recipes do not deal with the simple roasting, boiling or baking of food, but record the more complicated requirements for made dishes, or preserving, pickling and brewing – tasks not done every day, for which a source of reference would be needed. These recipes break down into the following groups:

Soups: two different versions of Pea Soup (one including other summer vegetables and the second some winter vegetables), Curry Soup (?Mulligatawny), Cowheel, White, Veal, and Swiss Soup Meagre [*sic*].

Meat: two recipes for Mock Turtle (using a calf's head), also Hashed Calves Head, Cabbage Pudding (leaves stuffed with minced meat), Scotch Collops, To Stew Pigeons Brown, Beefsteaks with Potatoes, Chicken Curry, Harrico of Mutton, Hogs Puddings, Sausages, Fried Patties, Risoles, Veal Cake.

Vegetables, cheese, etc.: A Rich Thick Cheese, Cheese Puddings, Toasted Cheese, Fricassee of Turnips, Rice to accompany meat dishes, Potato Yeast, Vegetable Pie, Macaroni, Raised Crust pastry and two recipes for Shortcrust.

Desserts, sweet puddings: Hartshorn Jelly, two recipes for Calves-feet Jelly (one adding wine), Lemon Pudding, two different Orange Puddings, Orange Jelly, A Fine Pancake, Quire-of-Paper Pancakes, Blanch Mange, Jaune Mange, Trifle, Almond Cream, Snow Cheese, Apple Snow, Baked Apple Pudding, Solid Custard, White Custard, A Two-penny Pudding (a thickened custard), two recipes for Rice Pudding, and another for Sweet Rice with Stewed Apples, New College Puddings (using breadcrumb) and four more different versions of Bread Pudding.

Cakes and biscuits: Plumb, Pound, and Carraway Cake, A Fine Cake, Wigs, Gingerbread, Wafers, Ollivers Biscuits, Lemon Cheesecakes, Almond Cheesecakes (these two are almost identical), Lemon Mince Pies, Cheesecake with Curd, Ratafia Cakes, Bolton Bunns, Biscuits.

Sauces: Wallnut Catchup, Soy, Mock Oyster Sauce, Bread Sauce, Gravy or Glaze, Curree Powder, two different sauces specifically for Carp and another five different sauces for fish in general.

Pickles: India Pickle, three versions of Lemon Pickle, Samphire, Dutch Plum or White Damson, Onions, Mushrooms, Melons, Cucumbers.

Chawton Cottage, where Martha Lloyd lived with Mrs George Austen, Cassandra and Jane.

Preserving: To Make Hams, To Cure Bacon (two similar versions), To Pickle Pork (two versions), Baked Buttock of Beef, Dried Ribs of Beef, Potted Beef, To Dry Mushrooms, To Keep Mushrooms as Fresh, To Preserve any Fruit, To Preserve Currants, Dried Gooseberries, To Candy Angelica, Damson Cakes, Gooseberry Cheese, Marmelade, Scotch Orange Marmelade.

Brewing: Mead, two recipes for Orange Wine (one adding Malaga raisins), Cowslip, Currant, Elderberry, Green Gooseberry Wine, two recipes for Noyeau (one using brandy with apricot kernels, the other gin with bitter almonds), Cherry Brandy, two recipes for Ginger Beer (one maturing more rapidly than the other), Orange or Lemon Juice (made into syrup), Gooseberry Vinegar, and Sugar, Raspberry, Pink, and Garlic Vinegars. (Surprisingly, no recipe for Spruce Beer is given – but perhaps Martha was so fond of it that she could make it from memory.)

The household recipes at the other end of Martha's book are mostly medical, with others for cosmetics, domestic purposes, and three for veterinary use. By today's standards they would nearly all be unnecessary to make and indeed some would be downright dangerous to use, so they are therefore not included among the modernised versions of the recipes which follow. They are listed here purely for their period interest.

Medical (all headed either 'To cure' or 'For the'): Swelled Neck, Consumption, Gravel, Hooping Cough, Ague, Worms (three different recipes), Sore Lips, Sore Eyes, Pain in the Side, Mad Dog Bite, Fever, Toothache; Eye Water, Steel Pills, Camphor Julep (two different recipes), Daffy's Elixir, Tincture of Guaiacum, Black Plaister, Black Draught, Saline Draught, Raspberry Vinegar (not the same recipe as that given in the other part of the book), Dr Turton's remedy for Colds, Dr Hartigan's Aperient Mixture and Dr Hartigan's Bark Mixture.

Veterinary: Wounds in Cattle, Mange in Horses or Dogs, The Staggers (a disease of the brain and spinal cord in cattle, which causes them to stagger – perhaps an early version of mad cow disease).

Cosmetics: Lavender Water, Coral Tooth Powder, Soap for Hands, Milk of Roses, Hard Pomatum, Rose Pomatum (two different recipes), Cold Cream (two different recipes).

Domestic: Blacking (two different recipes), Ink, Varnish for Tables, Blue or Buff Wash for Walls, To clean gilt things, To clean white silk stockings, To clean silks and gauzes, A Sweet Pot [pot-pourri], and another different Pot-Pourri mix.

Martha often included the names of those who had provided the recipes, and nearly all are also mentioned in Jane Austen's letters. Martha's sister Eliza, Mrs Fowle, offered one of the fish sauces, one of the Mock Turtle stews, a cure for bacon and a salve for sore lips; the latter's sister-in-law Mrs Charles Fowle gave an Orange Wine recipe, and old Aunt Jane Fowle knew how to make Curree Powder, while a niece's

11

A Carraway Cake

Take 3 p.d of flour, 2 p.d of Butter ~~rubbed~~
rubed into the flour an ounce & half of Carraway
seeds 12 spoonfuls of Milk, 12 spoonfuls of Yeast, 12
yolks of eggs 4 whites. beat all these well together
put them into your flour stiring it very well. let
it stand by the fire side a quarter of an hour to
rise. when the oven is hot strew in the carraway's
stiring it all the time. then butter your pan and
put in your cake. an hour and half will bake it.
N.B. Put in a pound of Sugar ————

To bake a buttock of Beef

Do a Buttock of Beef of 18 pounds take 2 q.d of common
Salt. half a p.d of coarse sugar & two oz: of Salt petre
let them be well rubbed in, and turn, the Beef every day
for a fortnight. then roll it up very tight with
beggars tape; put it into a deep pan and cover
it with equal parts of red wine and water. bake it
5 five hours take it out of the liquor when it is
cold. it will keep six or 8 weeks.

A page from the culinary section of Martha Lloyd's notebook of recipes.

husband, Mr Charles Dexter, gave one of the boot-blacking mixtures. Martha's young aunt Mrs Craven (second wife of the Revd John Craven) could also cure bacon, and gave the Cherry Brandy and one of the Ginger Beer brews, as well as the Green Gooseberry Cheese – to the latter entry Mrs Craven added cheerfully: 'good luck to your jamming'. Other friends in Berkshire were Mrs Dundas of Barton Court, near Kintbury (Cheese Pudding, Biscuits, Veal Cake); Mrs Hulbert of Speen (Shortcrust Pastry); Mrs Sawbridge of Welford, near Newbury (Solid Custard) and Mr Hartley of Bucklebury (Veal Soup, Gravy or Glaze, Bread Sauce, Fish Sauce) – this gentleman may perhaps be the same 'Mr Heartley' mentioned as one of Jane Austen's admirers in her letter of 14 January 1796.

On the other side of Martha's family connections, Mrs George Austen gave one of the Bread Pudding recipes, in easy-to-remember rhymes, as well as White Sauce for Carp, Raised Crust and Shortcrust Pastry. Mrs Henry Austen (probably Henry's first wife, Eliza de Feuillide) gave the gin-and-almond recipe for Noyeau, and Captain Austen (in actual fact more likely Frank's first wife Mary Gibson) gave another Fish Sauce and also the Milk of Roses cosmetic lotion; Mrs George Austen's niece Lady Williams gave one of the recipes for the popular Lemon Pickle. Lady Bridges (probably Edward Austen Knight's mother-in-law, who visited Chawton in 1814), offered one of the Cold Cream mixtures, and Miss Anne Sharp, the Godmersham governess, gave the dessert item of Dried Gooseberries. Friends in Hampshire were Mrs Lefroy (Raspberry Vinegar), Mrs Stephen Terry (Toothache remedy), Miss Debary (Scotch Orange Marmalade, Camphor Julep) and her sister Susan (one of the Bread Pudding recipes). Jane Austen usually preferred to avoid the Misses Debary, writing crossly to Cassandra on one occasion, 'I was as civil to them as their bad breath would allow me' – but for the Lloyd family they were neighbours at Ibthorpe and old friends from that period.

Another volume of domestic recipes, compiled by the Austens' friend Mrs Philip Lybbe Powys, is now preserved in the British Library (Add. Mss 42,173). In this it has been possible to find some more recipes emanating from the Austen family: Jane Austen's aunt Mrs Leigh-Perrot had a favourite Heart or Pound Cake, and young Lady Williams, before her early death in 1798, recorded recipes for Broild Eggs, Muffins, Pyramid Cream and Gooseberry Jam.

Recipes for a variety of Georgian dishes now follow; some of the items are taken from Martha Lloyd's manuscript book, some from Mrs Lybbe Powys, and others from published works of the period, in order to achieve a balanced selection from which complete menus can be composed.

Family Favourites

Swiss Soup Meagre

Take four Cabbage Lettuces, 1 Endive, Sorrel Spinnage, Cherville, Chives, Onions, Parsley, Beet leaves, Cucumbers sliced, Peas or Asparagus; let all these herbs be cut fine & no stalks put in, then put a quarter of a pd. of Butter in a Stew pan, shake over your herbs when they are in the Butter a small spoonful of flour & let them stew some time then pour in a quart of boiling Water & let it stew on till near dinner time; then add the yolks of three Eggs in a tea Cup of Cream & a Roll if you like it. Broth is better than so much water if you have it. If you have not all the vegetables above mention'd, it will be very good with what you have & a little Seville Orange juice if you like. (M.L., page 78.)

SERVES 6

10 oz/275 g varied salad leaves

8 oz/225 g cucumber

2 medium onions

4 oz/110 g/ ½ cup butter, chopped

6 oz/175 g/ ¾ cup shelled fresh young peas or frozen petits pois

1 teaspoon chopped fresh parsley

1 tablespoon chopped chives (fresh if possible)

1 tablespoon chopped fresh or ½ tablespoon dried mixed herbs

1 tablespoon flour

3 pints/1.7 litres/7 ½ cups vegetable stock

2 tablespoons soft white breadcrumbs, made without crust

3 egg yolks

4 fl oz/125 ml/ ½ cup single (light) cream

salt and pepper

Snip any tough stalks off the salad leaves, and shred any large leaves. Peel the cucumber, halve lengthways and slice. Peel the onions and chop them finely. Melt the chopped butter in a stew-pan, add the onions and cook gently for a couple of minutes. Add the cucumber, peas and all the leaves and herbs, and toss with a wooden spoon for a few moments. Sprinkle the flour over the greens, cover the pan and allow to simmer gently for 10 minutes, checking often that they are not burning. Add the stock and breadcrumbs, and continue cooking over low heat for another 20 minutes.

While cooking, whisk the egg yolks into the cream, and season with salt and pepper. When the soup is ready, take it off the heat, cool it for

2–3 minutes, then stir the cream mixture into it below the boil. Keep on the side of the stove until ready to serve.

Good with hot, dry toast or anchovy whets (page 66) – and not so very 'meagre'!

Curry Soup

Take a good Knuckle of Veal, put it up to boil with a Couple of Onions stuck with half a dozen Cloves, let it boil very gently till the Veal is tender, then take it out & cut it from the bone, into large dice, then take two large spoonfuls of rice; parch it before the fire, beat it in a Mortar & put it through a Lawn Sieve, take two ounces of Butter, the flour of Rice & a large Onion, choped small, put altogether into your stew pan, & put to them the broth & the Meat which you have cut from the bone, let simmer very gently till the meat is enough, then put into it two tea spoonfuls of Turmeric & season it with Chyan & black pepper to your taste. some rice boil'd dry must be serv'd up in a separate dish with this. The rice is to be boil'd in a Large quantity of Water and it must be thrown in when the water is boiling very fast & with it a handful of salt. (M.L., page 37.)

SERVES 6

4 pieces meaty veal knuckle

2 large onions, peeled

6 cloves

2 oz/50 g/4 tablespoons butter

2 level tablespoons brown rice flour

2 teaspoons ground turmeric

a few grains each Cayenne and black pepper

salt to taste

12 oz/350 g/2 cups hot, cooked long-grain rice

Put the knuckle pieces in a stew-pan with 3 pints/1.7 litres/7 ½ cups water. Stud the onions with 3 cloves each, add to the pan and bring to the boil. Cook slowly for 12–15 minutes, until the veal meat is tender. Put the knuckle pieces and 1 onion on a chopping board to cool slightly, then set the stew-pan, with the cooking water, on one side but close at hand.

Take the meat off the knuckle bones, carefully discarding the gristle together with the bones and spare onion. Cut the meat into small dice. Chop the cooled onion finely. In a bowl, blend the butter and rice flour, and add the chopped onion. Stir all these and the diced meat into the cooking liquid in the stew-pan. Simmer long enough to reheat the diced meat thoroughly, then stir in the turmeric, mixed pepper and salt to taste. Cook for another few minutes to blend the flavours before serving.

While the soup is cooking, boil or steam the long-grain rice. Hand it round in a bowl, with a small serving spoon, as a garnish for the soup.

Gravy and Glaze

Take a fore Shin of Beef, cut it in pieces, & lay it in a stew pan with six large onions – Turnip Carrot & two heads of Cellery & sweet herbs – set it on a stove & draw out the Gravy, let it be brown & all dried up, then put water to it, skim it very well & let it boil till very good Gravy – then strain it through a sieve, & when it is cold take off all the fat, & take any quantity you want, set it on the side of the stove without a Cover, & let it boil till it is like glue – put it on anything you wish to Glaze with a paste brush. (M.L., page 85.)

MAKES AT LEAST 3½ PINTS/2 LITRES/8¾ CUPS GRAVY

about 3 lb/1.5 kg beef bones or 2 lb/1 kg shin meat

about 1½ lb/700 g stewing lamb

good 2 lb/1 kg vegetables (onions, turnip, leek, carrot, celery), prepared for cooking

a few whole cloves and allspice berries

salt and pepper to taste

'Gravy' in Georgian times meant 'stock', based on bones and meat, vegetables (sometimes) and spices. Although beef and lamb were the commonest meats, almost any kind could be used. Mrs Glasse pointed out that 'fine cooks always (if they can) chop a partridge or two and put into gravies'. A Georgian 'broth' was also a stock or thin soup but made from only one or two kinds of meat to give it a particular flavour.

To make Martha's gravy, pre-heat the oven to about 400°F/200°C/Gas Mark 6. Brown the bones and meats in a baking-tin in the oven *without* the vegetables and with only a film of water covering the base of the tin. Then cut up the vegetables roughly, discarding any roots, and put them in a large stew-pan with the browned bones and meat and any juices in the baking-tin. Cover with 5 pints/2.8 litres/12 ½ cups water and simmer, covered, for about 2 hours. Strain, remove all the fat when cold, and refrigerate or freeze until wanted.

To use as a glaze, you will need to boil down a quantity of stock until only about 1 inch/2.5 cm is left. Leave it to cool, then brush the cooled, viscous glaze over any cold, cooked meats.

Vegetable Pie

Take as many Vegetables as are in season, Cabbage, Turnips, Carrots, Cucumbers, & Onions, fry them in Butter, when well fry'd drain, & season them with pepper & salt & lay them in layers in your dish or crust, cover them with a crust, have ready some good gravy to put into the pie when baked. It must not be put into a very hot oven. (M.L., page 72.)

SERVES 6

8 oz/225 g swede (rutabaga) or turnip, peeled and cut into large 'matchsticks'

8 oz/225 g parsnip, prepared like the swede

8 oz/225 g firm green cabbage, coarsely shredded

8 oz/225 g cucumber, quartered lengthways and cut across into fan-shaped slices (not too thin)

8 oz/225 g carrots, scraped and cut into rounds

6 oz/175 g onions, peeled and chopped

6 oz/175 g/ ¾ cup unsalted butter, chopped

1 tablespoon frying oil

salt and freshly ground black pepper

8 oz/225 g puff pastry

1 egg, lightly beaten

10 fl oz/275 ml/1 ¼ cups vegetable stock (can be made with ½ stock cube: see method)

Martha suggested using any seasonal garden vegetable for her pie, then specified 5 kinds. I have in fact used 6, because the quantities filled a 2-pint/1.1-litre/5-cup deep pie dish neatly, but you can adapt them to any type of vegetables you want to use.

Parboil the swede and parsnip shreds together, and in another pan the cabbage and cucumber. Parboil the carrot rounds separately. Drain all the vegetables, keeping them separate, and pour the cooking water into a measuring jug.

In a frying-pan (skillet) or wok, fry the onions in about 1 oz/25 g/ 2 tablespoons butter and all the oil until just starting to soften. Add the swede and parsnip shreds and toss until tender. Spread them over the base of a 2-pint/1.1-litre/5-cup deep pie dish and sprinkle with seasoning. Put the cabbage and cucumber in the pan, add a little more butter and fry until tender, spread them over the swede and parsnip and season them. Fry, add and season the carrots likewise. They should fill the dish.

Set the oven to heat to 400°F/200°C/Gas Mark 6. Roll out the pastry into an oval about 1 1/4 inches/3 cm bigger than the top of the pie dish. Brush the rim of the dish with egg. Cut a strip of pastry from the edge of the rolled-out shape and fit it over the rim. Brush it with egg, then fit the pastry sheet over it to cover the pie. Flute or crimp the edge to seal it. Make triangular slits in the pie to let steam escape, and decorate it with small shapes cut from the pastry trimmings. Bake it in the oven for 12–15 minutes, then reduce the temperature to 325°F/170°C/Gas Mark 3 and bake for another 10 minutes or until the pastry is cooked through.

While cooking the pie, make a 'gravy'. Measure the reserved vegetable cooking water and add half a vegetable or garlic-and-herb stock cube. Heat gently to dissolve it. Add enough simmering water to make 10 fl oz/275 ml/1 1/4 cups liquid and taste to check the seasoning. Pour some 'gravy' into the pie through one of the slit holes and serve the rest separately.

Fricassee of Turnips

*Cut your Turnips in dice, when boiled and put a little cream to them thicken'd
with flour & add a little lump Sugar to your taste. (M.L., page 51.)*

SERVES 6

2 lb/1 kg small young turnips

salt and white pepper

8 fl oz/225 ml/1 cup single (light) cream

1 tablespoon plain (all-purpose) flour

½ tablespoon white sugar

pinch of grated nutmeg (optional)

Top and tail the turnips, and peel any with coarse or blemished skins.
Cut into ½-inch/1-cm dice. Put at once into a pan of cold water, add a
little salt and bring gently to the boil. Cook for 10–15 minutes until tender
but not soft.

While the turnips are cooking, gradually blend the cream into the
flour, making a smooth paste and then a cream. Stir it in a small
saucepan over gentle heat just until slightly thickened; season and fold in
the sugar and the spice if you are using it. Drain the turnips and put them
in a warmed serving dish. Then fold in the warmed cream and serve.

Ragoo of Celery with Wine

Wash and make a bunch of celery very clean, cut it in pieces about two inches long, put it into a stew-pan with just as much water as will cover it, tie three or four blades of mace, two or three cloves, about twenty corns of whole pepper in a muslin bag loose, put it into a stew-pan, a little onion, a little bundle of sweet herbs; cover it close, and let it stew softly till tender; then take out the spice, onion, and sweet herbs, put in half an ounce of truffles and morels, two spoonfuls of catchup, a gill of red wine, a piece of butter as big as an egg, rolled in flour, six farthing French rolls, season with salt to your palate, stir it all together, cover it close, and let it stew till the sauce is thick and good; take care that the rolls do not break, shake your pan often; when it is enough dish it up, and garnish with lemon. The yolks of six hard eggs, or more, put in with the rolls, will make it a fine dish. This for a first course.
If you would have it white, put in white wine instead of red, and some cream for a second course. (H.G. 1796, fac. 1971, page 228.)

SERVES 6

1 large head celery

3 blades mace

3 whole cloves

12–16 black peppercorns

4 oz/110 g onion, peeled and cut in large pieces

1 bouquet garni

1 × 20 g packet dried porcini mushrooms, soaked and drained

1 ½ tablespoons tomato ketchup (with red wine) or mushroom ketchup (with white wine)

5 fl oz/150 ml/⅔ cup red or white wine

about 2 oz/50 g beurre manié made with 1 oz/25 g each softened butter and flour

2 fl oz/50 ml/¼ cup single (light) cream (with white wine)

salt and pepper

4 small bridge rolls, sliced like French bread and toasted

6 whole hard-boiled egg yolks

Wash the celery well, cut off the root and leaves, and discard any damaged parts. Cut the good stems into 1-inch/2.5-cm lengths.

Put the celery into a saucepan with enough water to cover it completely. Add the spices and onion tied in a square of muslin, and the bouquet garni, but no salt. Cover the pan closely and simmer for 30–40 minutes or until the celery is tender.

Drain the contents of the pan into a colander (strainer) set over a large bowl. Remove the spice bag and bouquet garni and return 10 fl oz/ 275 ml/1¼ cups liquid from the bowl to the pan. Add the mushrooms, ketchup and wine and simmer for 3–4 minutes, until the mushrooms soften. Remove the pan from the heat and stir in the beurre manié in small spoonfuls. Return to the heat and simmer until the sauce thickens. Stir in the cream if you are using it. Replace the celery, and heat it through in the sauce. Season to taste, transfer to a heated serving dish and keep warm.

In the old recipe the sliced rolls and hard-boiled egg yolks are added to the thickened sauce. However, the dish will look more dramatic if you surround the celery with golden overlapping slices of bridge roll and pile the whole egg yolks on top of the dish as a garnish.

Herb Pudding

Take a quart of grots, and steep them in warm water half an hour. Take a pound of hog's lard, and cut it into little bits. Take of spinach, beets, parsley and leeks, a handful of each; three large onions chopped small, and three sage leaves cut fine. Put in a little salt, mix all well together, and tie it close. It will require to be taken up in boiling, to loosen the string a little. (J.F. 7th edn, page 198.)

SERVES 4–6

4 oz/110 g/1 cup self-raising flour, sifted

4 oz/110 g/1 cup fine oatmeal

2 oz/50 g/1 cup soft white breadcrumbs

5 oz/150 g/1¼ cups shredded suet or pork dripping

a good fistful of finely chopped spinach and other green leaves, including parsley and green of young leek (use enough leaves to tint the pudding)

1 medium onion, peeled and finely chopped

1 teaspoon chopped fresh sage or ½ teaspoon dried sage

½ teaspoon salt

Until potatoes replaced it in our daily diet, a plain or savoury pudding was often served with meat, or as a 'filler' before it in poorer country households. Flour and oatmeal make an easier pudding to manage than hulled, pounded oats for this basic dish.

Stir together all the ingredients and mix to a stiff dough with cold water. You can boil your pudding in a floured cloth, in the old way, if you like. Tie it securely, leaving room inside the cloth for the pudding to swell, and boil it for 2–2½ hours, topping up the pan with boiling water when needed. Alternatively turn the mixture into a greased 1½-pint/850-ml/3⅔-cup pudding basin and cover securely. Stand the basin on a trivet in a saucepan and pour enough boiling water into the pan to come half-way up the sides of the basin. Put a lid on the pan and steam for 3 hours.

In the latter case, serve the pudding in the basin with a white napkin tied round it, or let it stand for 10 minutes, then turn it out on to a platter and cut it like a cake. It is excellent with any roasted meat or game bird instead of potatoes or stuffing, especially when served with the pan juices or gravy.

How to Dress Salads

The Method which I most approve of for dressing a Sallad is, after we have duly proportion'd the Herbs, to take two thirds Oil Olive, one third true Vinegar, some hard Eggs cut small, both the Whites and Yolks, a little Salt and some Mustard, all which must be well mix'd and pour'd over the Sallad, having first cut the large Herbs, such as Sallery, Endive, or Cabbage-Lettuce, but none of the small ones: then mix all these well together, that it may be ready just when you want to use it, for the Oil will make it presently soften, and lose its briskness. Onions should always be kept in reserve, because it is not every one that likes their relish, nor is Oil agreeable to every one; but where Oil is not liked, the Yolks of hard Eggs, bruis'd and mix'd with the Vinegar, may be used as above. The difficulty of getting good Oil in England is, I suppose, the reason why every one does not admit it; for I was once of opinion I could never like it: but when I was once persuaded to taste such as was of the best sort, I could never after like a Sallad without it.
(R.B. 1736, fac. 1980, pages 95–6.)

MAKES 8 FL OZ/225 ML/1 CUP

4 fl oz/125 ml/½ cup olive oil

2 fl oz/50 ml/¼ cup white wine vinegar

¼ teaspoon made English mustard

good pinch of sea salt

1 hard-boiled egg

In a measuring jug, whisk together the oil, vinegar, mustard and salt. Shell the egg and chop it roughly, then process it in an electric blender so that the white is finely chopped. Combine with the dressing and refrigerate until needed. Whisk again to blend the ingredients just before using.

For a smoother texture, sieve in 3 hard-boiled yolks instead of using a whole egg.

Macaroni

Stew a quarter of a pd. of the pipe Macaroni in milk & water until tis tender, then lay it upon top of a sive to drain. – Put it into a stew pan with two large spoonfuls of grated parmesan Cheese, a quarter of a pint of Cream, a small piece of Butter & some salt – Stew it gently till the whole seems well done, then put it into a dish, strew grated Parmesan Cheese over it, & brown it with a Salamander or in a Dutch Oven – It may be done with gravy instead of Cream if prefered.
(M.L., page 94.)

SERVES 2

4 oz/110 g/1 cup dried macaroni

equal quantities of milk and water for cooking (see method)

about 2 oz/50 g/½ cup freshly grated Parmesan cheese
(see note at end of method)

5 fl oz/150 ml/⅔ cup single (light) cream or gravy (see page 42)

1 level tablespoon butter

salt and pepper

Cook the macaroni until tender in plenty of gently boiling milk and water; keep your eye on it to forestall any chance of it boiling over, and stir round sometimes to prevent the pieces of pasta sticking together.

When it is cooked *al dente*, drain the pasta in a colander or round-based sieve (strainer). Then return it to the dry pan. Scatter in about two-thirds of the cheese, and add the cream or gravy, butter and seasoning. Replace the pan over very gentle heat, and toss the pasta to melt the cheese and combine the whole mixture, again taking care not to let it stick to the pan. As soon as the cheese has melted, transfer the pasta to a shallow flameproof dish, scatter the remaining Parmesan on top and slip the dish under a pre-heated grill (broiler) for 3–4 minutes to brown the top. Serve at once.

This seemingly simple and remarkably quick dish is deceptive in one way. It *demands* to be made with *fresh* Parmesan, not with cheese from a carton.

The dish must have placed poor Mr Woodhouse in a sad dilemma as to whether cream or gravy would be the least harmful moistening medium.

To feed 6 people, use 12 oz/350 g/3 cups macaroni, moistened with about 10 fl oz/275 ml/1 ¼ cups cream or gravy. Add a little savory or marjoram if your digestion permits it.

Salmon, Pike, Carps or Fresh Cod in Corbullion

First scale, draw, and cleanse your Fish very well; then lay your Fish into a Corbullion, made as follows: Take one Part Wine, one Part Vinegar, and two Parts Water; season it well with Salt, whole Pepper, Cloves, Mace and Ginger; put in some Onions, Horse-radish, a good Faggot of sweet Herbs, and a few Bay-leaves; pour this cold all over your Fish, and let there be enough of it to boil it in; let it lie an Hour in this Corbullion, and then take out your Fish, and set your Corbullion on to boil; and when it boils up, put in your Fish; when boil'd enough, take it out, and drain it well; dish it, and lay some other small Fish about it, either boil'd or fry'd, or broil'd, and garnish with Horse-radish and slic'd Lemon.
(C.C. 1730, fac. 1984, page 69.)

SERVES 6

1 fish, about 3 lb/1.4 kg, and 2 inches/5 cm thick, gutted and scaled

spice bundle containing 5 black peppercorns; 2 whole cloves;
1 large blade mace; 1 slice fresh ginger root; 1 shallot, halved;
2 red radishes, halved; a sprig each of fresh thyme, marjoram and rosemary;
2 bay leaves

10 fl oz/275 ml/1 ¼ cups medium-dry white wine

3 tablespoons white wine vinegar

sea salt to taste

garnish of cooked prawns if serving hot or of sliced radishes and
preserved lemon slices if serving cold

Any fairly large fish was generally 'boiled': that is, poached in a fish-kettle, having first been wrapped in a cloth. An oval pot-roaster or a stew-pan is suitable for most fish; one measuring 14 × 9 inches/36 ×

23 cm is a convenient size, holding about 7 pints/4 litres/17 ½ cups liquid when brimful.

Ask the fishmonger to gut and scale the fish. Prepare the spices. A square of butter muslin makes a good 'bundle'. Put in the centre the dried spices, ginger root, shallot, radishes and herbs, then tie the opposite points together.

Wrap the cleaned fish in another piece of muslin folded over on top to make unwrapping easy. Put it on a trivet or serving dish in a stew-pan or pot-roaster. Add the spice bundle, then pour the liquids, including about 4 pints/2.3 litres/10 cups water, over the lot – the fish should be just covered. Add salt to taste and leave to soak for about an hour.

Remove the wrapped fish and gently bring the cooking liquid to simmering point. Replace the fish and poach very gently for about 15 minutes. Unwrap to check whether it is done. When it is, lift it out, and drain it well.

You can serve it hot, preferably skinned, with some prawns and the wine sauce on page 73, or cold with the radish and preserved lemon slices, new potatoes and a salad. Substitute scrapings of fresh horseradish for the radishes if you have any.

Plaice and Flounders

Run your knife all along upon the bone on the back-side of the fish, and raise the flesh on both sides, from the head to the tail. Then take out the bone clear, and cut your fish in six collops. Dry it well, sprinkle it with salt, dredge them with flour, and fry them in a pan of hot beef-dripping, so that the fish may be crisp. Take it out of the pan, and keep it warm before the fire; then clean the pan, and put into it some minced oysters, and their liquor strained, some white wine, a little grated nutmeg, and three anchovies. Having stewed these up together, put in half a pound of butter, and then your fish. Toss them well together, dish them on sippets, and pour the sauce over them. Garnish with the yolks of eggs, boiled hard, and minced, and lemon sliced. In this manner you may fricasee salmon, or any firm fish.
(J.F. 7th edn., page 100.)

SERVES 6

3 medium-sized plaice or 2 × 1 lb/450 g lemon soles, gutted, skinned and filleted

6 canned anchovy fillets

a little milk

salt

flour for dredging

oil or butter for frying

6 steamed oysters, diced (see page 92)

4 fl oz/125 ml/ ½ cup dry white wine

pinch of grated nutmeg

4 oz/110 g/ ½ cup unsalted butter

lightly fried or toasted bread slices without crusts
Garnish

2 or 3 hard-boiled egg yolks

lemon slices

Ask the fishmonger to gut, skin and fillet the fish. Chop the anchovies and soak them in a little milk to de-salt and soften them. Cut the fish fillets across into 2 or 3 pieces. Dry them, then sprinkle them with salt and flour. Fry them in the oil or butter, turning once, until cooked. Keep warm.

Clean the pan, then add to it the oysters, their liquor, the white wine, nutmeg and soaked anchovies. Add the unsalted butter in small pieces, melt it, swirl it around and put in the fried fish. Have ready the fried bread or toast slices on a dish. Put the fish and its garnishes on top, sprinkle with crumbled egg yolk and serve with lemon slices and the butter sauce.

A Harrico of Mutton

Cut a Neck of Mutton into Steaks flour them & fry them brown on each side. Put into your stew pan a piece of Butter & two spoonfuls of flour, & let it simmer together till it is of a light brown keeping it stirring all the time add to it some good Gravy & let it boil up, then put in your steaks, & Turnips & Carrots, & let it stew one hour pepper & salt it to your taste & two spoonfuls of Catchup. – When done, if Greasy mix some flour with cold water and put in to it, but let it only boil up once afterwards. (M.L., page 66.)

SERVES 6

6 or 8 lamb chops for frying

flour for dusting

unsalted butter and oil for frying

1 oz/25 g/2 tablespoons butter for the sauce

2 tablespoons seasoned flour for the sauce

about 1 pint/575 ml/2 ½ cups gravy (see page 42) or good lamb stock

2 tablespoons mushroom ketchup

3 medium-sized turnips, peeled and cut into small pieces (parsnips or a small swede (rutabaga) can be used instead)

2 medium-sized carrots, peeled and cut into small pieces

salt and freshly ground black pepper

Trim the chops, removing skin and excess fat. Dust them with flour on both sides, and fry them in the unsalted butter and oil until lightly browned. Put them aside to drain on soft kitchen paper (paper towels).

In a flameproof casserole or a stew-pan with a tight-fitting lid, melt the butter for the sauce, add the seasoned flour and stir over low heat until fawn-coloured. Add, gradually, about half the gravy or stock and bring to boiling point. Stir in the mushroom ketchup. Then add the chops and vegetables, top up the sauce with gravy or stock if needed so that it covers the meat and vegetables and put a tight lid on the casserole. Simmer gently for about 1 hour, adding a little more gravy or stock if necessary during the cooking.

Adjust the seasoning if required, then serve from the casserole. If necessary, skim or blot the surface to remove any fat before serving. If your chops are well trimmed and the sauce has completely blended, it should not be at all greasy.

Jugged Steaks with Potatoes

Take rump Steakes, beat them well, pepper & salt them, then take a soup-pot, put at the bottom a little fresh butter, a row of Stakes, a row of Potatoes, & so on till tis full, then fill some gravy or broth just enough to cover it, let it stew for three hours, then strain it all off & skim all the fat from it, thicken it up with butter & flour, then put it over the steakes again, give it one boil up, & taste if salt enough.
(M.L., page 32.)

SERVES 6

2–3 ½ lb / 1–1.6 kg rump steak, cut into 6–8 serving slices and trimmed

salt and pepper

2 oz / 50 g / 4 tablespoons unsalted butter, chilled

2 lb / 1 kg boiling potatoes, peeled and sliced (or as many as you need to fill the dish – see method)

well-flavoured beef stock to cover the meat and potatoes

beurre manié as needed (see method)

Pre-heat the oven to 275°F/140°C/Gas Mark 1. Choose a sturdy but decorative flameproof casserole. Beat out the steaks with a mallet or cutlet bat, and season them on both sides. Slice the butter thinly and cover the base of the casserole with some or all of it, then cover the butter with a layer of meat, followed by a layer of potato slices. Repeat the layers until the casserole is almost full, then fill it up with stock. Cover tightly and cook in the oven for 2 ½–3 hours, until the meat is tender. Add a little more stock if needed to prevent the dish drying out on top.

At the end of the cooking time, drain off the liquid into a measuring jug and skim it thoroughly. Heat it gently in a saucepan almost to boiling point, adding 1 ½ oz / 40 g beurre manié for each 10 fl oz / 275 ml / 1 ¼ cups liquid while doing so. Make sure that you will have enough sauce for all the steaks; add a bit more stock if you need to. Then taste for seasoning. Simmer the sauce for a few minutes to thicken it, then pour it back over the dish. Reheat it without boiling for a moment or two just before serving.

Potatoes were being used quite widely in Jane Austen's day in savoury *and* sweet dishes, but were still unusual enough to arouse curiosity.

Beef-steak Pudding

Prepare some fine steaks; . . . roll them with fat between; and if you approve shred
*onion, add a very little. Lay a paste of suet in a basin, and put in the rollers of
steaks, cover the basin with a paste, and pinch the edges to keep the gravy in. Cover
with a cloth tied close, and let the pudding boil slowly, but for a length of time.*
(M.R. 1806 edn, page 145.)

SERVES 6

1 ¾ lb/800 g casserole steak, thinly sliced

a little soft dripping

4 oz/110 g/1 cup self-raising flour

4 oz/110 g/1 cup fine oatmeal

3 oz/75 g/1 ½ cups soft white breadcrumbs

4 oz/110 g/1 cup shredded suet

1 teaspoon salt

2 tablespoons shredded onion

4 tablespoons beef stock or gravy (see page 42)

Flatten the meat with a cutlet bat. Brush it with dripping, then cut it into
small pieces.

In a large bowl, mix together the flour, oatmeal, breadcrumbs, suet
and salt, and mix to a stiff dough with about 6 fl oz/175 ml/¾ cup cold
water. Shape it into a block and cut off a quarter of it for a lid; set this
quarter aside.

Grease the inside of a 2-pint/1.1-litre/5-cup basin. Roll the larger
piece of pastry into a round about 2 inches/5 cm bigger than the top of
the greased basin. On a floured surface, fold it in half, then in half again,
making a fan shape. Place it in the basin, point side down. Then unfold it,
making a lining for the basin. Fill the steak pieces and onion into the
centre; they should fill most of the basin. Fold the top uncovered pastry
inwards over the meat. Trickle half the stock or gravy into the middle of
the pudding.

Roll the reserved pastry into a round to fit the top of the basin. Damp
the edges of the lining pastry and lid, then seal them together. Cover the
pudding with a circle of greased greaseproof paper (baking parchment),
then with a larger circle of greased foil; pleat it to fit neatly over the sides
of the basin.

To help the pudding cook evenly, and to help you take it out of the
saucepan afterwards, use a saucepan 2 inches/5 cm bigger in diameter

than the pudding basin. Place a folded tea-towel (dish-towel) or a long strip of doubled foil centrally across the inside centre of the base and up each side of the saucepan. Put the pudding in the saucepan, so that it rests on the tea-towel or foil, and pour in enough *boiling* water to come half-way up the basin's sides. Cover the pan with a lid or plate and boil gently for 2½–3 hours; check the water level from time to time and top up with extra boiling water if required.

Remove the pan from the heat and leave to stand, uncovered, for a few minutes. Separately heat the stock not yet used. Take the pudding out of the pan. Carefully cut a wedge from the pastry lid and pour in any more stock required. Replace the pastry wedge.

Serve the pudding in its basin, wrapped in a white napkin.

A Receipt to Curry after the Indian Manner

Cut two Chickens as for fricasseeing, wash them clean & put them in a stew pan with as much water as will cover them, with a large spoonful of salt sprinkle them & let them boil till tender covered close all the time, skim them well; when boiled enough take up the Chickens & put the liquor of them in a pan, then put half a pound of fresh butter in the pan & brown it a little, put into it two cloves of garlic & a large onion sliced & let these all fry till brown often shaking the pan, then put in Chickens & sprinkle over them two or three spoonfuls of curry powder, then cover them close & let the Chickens do till brown frequently shaking the Pan, then put in the Liquor the Chickens were boiled in & let all stew till tender. If acid is agreeable squeeze the juice of a Lemon or Orange into it. (M.L., pages 51–2.)

SERVES 6

6–8 fleshy chicken joints

pinch of salt

4 oz/110 g/½ cup unsalted butter

2 cloves garlic, peeled and chopped

6 oz/175 g onions, peeled and chopped

2 tablespoons Curree Powder (see page 103)

juice of 1 Seville orange or lemon (optional)

Wipe the chicken joints and put them in a stew-pan with enough water to cover and a small pinch of salt. Put the lid on the pan and cook gently till tender. Transfer the joints to a plate; keep the cooking liquid aside.

Melt the butter in a pan which will hold all the ingredients: bring it to sizzling point, then add the garlic and onions and sauté until browned. Add the chicken joints and 'curree powder', and stir, shaking the pan, for 3–4 minutes until the chicken pieces are well coated. Stir in 1 pint/ 575 ml/2 ½ cups of the cooking liquid, then cover the pan and simmer until the mixture is well heated through. Taste for seasoning and stir in a little orange or lemon juice if you wish.

It is worth freezing some Seville orange juice when the fruit is in season for this and similar dishes which welcome a tangy flavour.

Lady Williams's Muffins

half a Gallon of Flour, half a pint of Yeast, put as much water as will make it about the thickness of paste, stir a little salt into it, and beat it well over night. ye next morning lay a clean Cloth on a table and flour it, then turn ye past out of the pan and make them up with your hands into small flat Cakes. they must be baked upon an Iron *plate over ye Fire and when half done turn'd. (L.P., page 54.)*

MAKES 8

2 tablespoons softened butter

7 fl oz/200 ml/just under 1 cup whole milk

½ oz/15 g compressed fresh yeast

½ teaspoon white sugar

1 tablespoon sea salt

1 lb/450 g strong plain flour (see note at end of method)

rice flour for dusting

In well-to-do Regency England, the plain loaves and buns of the past gave place to fancy breads which were more like pastries. Even the dough for the small breads called muffins might be enriched with eggs and butter.

However, not all housewives 'fell' for the luxury foodstuffs. Mrs Lybbe Powys and her friend Lady Williams used only flour, water, yeast and salt to make muffins. Their muffins were more like modern English ones, fairly solid, flat-topped unflavoured buns made with yeast. In updating their recipe, therefore, I have compromised, following more closely our greatest exponent of modern yeast cookery, Elizabeth David. I have used, for instance, modern strong flour, and Mrs David's suggestion of rice flour for handling the dough, but not the eggs which made some Regency muffins more like teacakes.

In a measuring jug, melt the butter in 7 fl oz/200 ml/just under 1 cup fairly hot water, then add the milk. Put the yeast and sugar in a small bowl and blend in about 2 tablespoons of the liquid to 'cream' them. Mix the salt into the flour and warm it well; for instance, in a microwave oven.

When the flour is warm, add the milk and water from the jug, and then the creamed yeast; I find it blends in better if added last. Stir the mixture vigorously until it forms a single, very soft mass. Cover the bowl and leave it at kitchen temperature for 1 hour.

Dust your worktop with rice flour, and turn the muffin mixture on to it. Pat it into an oblong about 1½ inches/4 cm thick. Then cut it into 8 squares and round off the corners with your hands. This way you get round muffins with tidy flat tops. Cover them with a cloth and leave them to prove for about 40 minutes.

Cook the muffins on a flat surface, such as a chef's *iron* baking-sheet, not in a frying-pan (skillet). Oil or grease it lightly and place it over low heat; muffins scorch quickly. Cook no more than 4 muffins at a time and wrap them in a cloth as soon as they are ready. All that remains is to toast them on each side and then split and butter them – and tie your napkin under your chin!

Strong *brown* flour makes delicious muffins, especially good with pickles for picnics.

Pyramid Creams

two ounces Hartshorn shavings, put in a jar stopt quite close, and set in a pot of
boiling water till dissolved. one ounce sweet Almonds blanch'd & beat half a
Lemon 2 ounces sugar sifted pour it into ale glasses & when Cold turn them out on
your dish, cut Lemon peel in Shape of leaves and stick 3 or 4 in each pyramid.
(L.P., page 54.)

SERVES 6

1 pint/575 ml/2 ½ cups white wine mixed with 10 fl oz/275 ml/1 ¼ cups water

4 teaspoons powdered gelatine

2 tablespoons strained lemon juice

2 oz/50 g/ ⅓ cup caster (superfine) sugar

½ oz/15 g almond flakes, pounded into small bits but not powdered

1 large piece candied lemon peel, grated, or the grated rind of
1 large fresh lemon mixed with a little sugar

6 tablespoons thick double (heavy) cream

I have based my interpretation of this recipe on Mrs E. Raffald's recipes for Hartshorn Jelly and Cream. For general use, 1 oz/25 g hartshorn scrapings appears to have set 15 fl oz/425 ml/2 cups liquid. In a good many recipes for dessert 'creams' the real cream seems only to have been poured over the completed dish. Hartshorn, like ivory, has no perceptible flavour.

Bring the wine and water to just below simmering point and tip in the gelatine. Off the heat, stir until the gelatine dissolves completely, then stir in the lemon juice and caster sugar. Make sure that the sugar is dissolved. Taste for sweetness, then pour into 6 × 4-fl-oz/120-ml/ ½-cup flute-shaped glasses and leave until about to set. Stir in half the pounded almond flakes. Refrigerate until half-set, then stir in the rest of the flakes. Refrigerate again until fully set, and then for 24 hours longer to stiffen the jelly.

If the jelly is firm enough, you can turn it out by dipping the glasses briefly into hot water. Whether you do or not, sprinkle the top surface with grated candied lemon peel, or fresh lemon rind and sugar. Serve with the cream.

Apple Pie

Pare and core the fruit, having wiped the outside; which, with the cores, boil with a little water till it tastes well; strain, and put a little sugar, and a bit of bruised cinnamon, and simmer again. In the mean time place the apples in a dish, a paste being put round the edge; when one layer is in, sprinkle half the sugar and shred lemon-peel, and squeeze some juice, or a glass of cider if the apples have lost their spirit; put in the rest of the apples, sugar, and the liquor that you have boiled. Cover with paste. You may add some butter when cut, if eaten hot; or put quince-marmalade, orange-paste, or cloves, to flavour. (M.R. 1806 edn, page 157.)

SERVES 6

12 oz/350 g shortcrust pastry

2 lb/1 kg Bramley apples

3 oz/75 g/ ½ cup caster (superfine) sugar

½ cinnamon stick

grated rind of ½ lemon

2 cloves

egg wash for glazing

2–3 teaspoons softened butter (see method)

Roll out the pastry to fit the top of a 1¾-pt/1-litre/4½-cup English pie dish or deep pie plate with 1½ inches/4 cm extra pastry all round when inverted. Leave to 'rest'.

Pare and core the fruit. Put the peel and cores in a pan with about 4 fl oz/125 ml/ ½ cup water. Simmer down to about 2 fl oz/50 ml/ ¼ cup liquid, then strain the liquid into a clean pan. Add a sprinkling of the sugar and the cinnamon, and simmer for 2 minutes more. Remove from the heat and leave to infuse.

Place a pie funnel in the centre of the pie dish. Slice the apples and arrange half in the dish. Sprinkle with half the remaining sugar and the grated lemon rind, then top with the rest of the fruit and sugar, the cloves and the strained infused liquid.

Set the oven to heat to 400°F/200°C/Gas Mark 6. Cut off the outside 1 inch/2.5 cm of rolled-out pastry. Moisten the rim of the dish and fit over it the strip of pastry which you have cut off. Moisten the top of the strip, especially where the ends overlap. Fold the pastry cover over a rolling pin so that you can lift it easily and lay it on top of the pie. Trim any wide overhang. Seal the pastry strip and top rim of the pie cover with the tines of a fork or by fluting or scalloping the edge. Make arrowhead slits in the pastry cover and raise the triangular tongues of pastry slightly. Brush the surface of the pastry with egg wash. If you wish, add decorative pastry leaves or emblems to the pastry cover and brush a little extra egg wash over them too.

Bake the pie for 35–40 minutes. Cover it loosely with wetted grease-proof paper if it starts to get too brown. If you want to serve it hot, cut one pastry wedge out of the cover and drop in the softened butter.

Solid Custard

In a quart of Milk boil an oz. of Isinglass until the latter is dissolved, then strain it through a Sive, let it stand a short time, add the Yolks of five Eggs well beaten, mix them with the Milk & set it on the fire until it is as thick as a rich boiled Custard, sweeten & put it into a Mould to prepare it for the Table – A few Bitter Almonds or a Bay leaf will improve the flavour very much. (M.L., page 90.)

MAKES 2 PINTS/1.1 LITRES/5 CUPS

2 pints/1.1 litres/5 cups milk

2 fresh bay leaves or 1 dried bay leaf

1 ½ tablespoons powdered gelatine

4 egg yolks, beaten

1–2 tablespoons caster (superfine) sugar

fresh bay leaves to decorate (optional)

Bring the milk with the bay leaves or leaf almost to scalding point in a saucepan, scatter on the gelatine and stir until it dissolves. Leave to stand for a few minutes, then take out the bay and whisk in the egg yolks and sugar. Heat the mixture *very* slowly, stirring occasionally, so that it thickens before reaching the boil. Transfer it to a decorative mould or dish and leave it to get thoroughly cold before serving. This may take several hours. Decorate with 1 or 2 fresh bay leaves if you like.

For a pouring custard, reduce or omit the gelatine.

A Receipt for a Pudding
(Bread Pudding)

If the Vicar you treat, / You must give him to eat, / A pudding to hit his affection; / And to make his repast / By the canon of taste, / Be the present receipt your direction.

first take two pounds of Bread, / Be the crumb only weigh'd, / For crust the good house-wife refuses; / The proportion you'll guess, / May be made more, or less, / To the size that each family chuses.

Then its sweetness to make / Some currants you take / And Sugar of each half a pound / Be not Butter forgot / And the quantity sought / Must the same with your currants be found.

Cloves & Mace you will want, / With rose water I grant, / And more savory things if well chosen; / Then to bind each ingredient, / Youll find it expedient, / of Eggs to put in half a dozen.

Some milk dont refuse it, / But boiled ere you use it, / A proper hint this for its maker; / And the whole when compleat, / In a pan clean and neat, / With care recommend to the baker.

In praise of this pudding, / I vouch it a good one, / Or should you suspect a fond word; / To every Guest, / Perhaps it is best, / Two puddings should smoke on the board.

Two puddings! — yet no, / For if one will do, / The other comes in out of season; / And these lines but obey, / nor can anyone say, / That this pudding's without rhyme or reason. (M.L., page 7).

SERVES 6

10 oz/275 g/5 cups soft white breadcrumbs

4 oz/110 g/½ cup butter

4 oz/110 g/¾ cup light soft brown sugar

2 small eggs, lightly beaten

1 tablespoon rose-water

1 teaspoon grated lemon rind

pinch each of ground cloves and mace

¼ teaspoon salt

small pinch of white pepper

4 oz/110 g/¾ cup currants

about 2 fl oz/50 ml/¼ cup milk to mix

Set the oven to heat to 350°F/180°C/Gas Mark 4. Dry the breadcrumbs on a baking-sheet in the bottom of the oven for a few minutes, turning them over to dry them evenly.

Cream together the butter and sugar, and beat in the eggs and rose-water. Mix in the crumbs with a fork, then add all the other dry ingredients. Add the currants last. Mix with enough milk to give the pudding a fairly crumbly texture.

Turn the pudding into a lightly greased 1½-pint/850-ml/3⅔-cup heatproof soufflé dish. Cover with foil. Bake for 1–1¼ hours, or until the pudding tests clean with a skewer. Leave to stand in the dish for 10 minutes. Serve warm from the dish if you like, with custard or cream. Alternatively cool in the dish, loosen from the sides with a knife and turn out for serving cold. This mixture makes a good, light bread pudding when baked.

Mrs Dundas's Biscuits

Take two oz: of lard or butter, & two lb. of flour, mix them well together stiff with a little cold water, work or knead them very well roll your biscuits very thin, & prick them exceedingly, bake them on tins in a very quick oven, looking constantly at them or they will scorch. (M.L., page 60.)

MAKES 10–12

½ oz/15 g/1 tablespoon butter

8 oz/225 g/2 cups flour

good pinch of salt

Pre-heat the oven to 425°F/220°C/Gas Mark 7; also grease and flour 2 baking-trays lightly, or cover with baking parchment.

Mix the butter into the flour with the salt; in a food processor is the easiest way. When the mixture is like fine breadcrumbs, add a little cold water: you will need about 2 tablespoons altogether, but add only a little at a time and work the liquid into the dry goods very thoroughly after each addition, until you have a stiff dough.

Roll out the dough as thinly as you possibly can, and cut it into rounds with a 4-inch/10-cm cutter. Prick each one all over with a fork. Place them on the baking-trays and put them straight in the oven, near the top. Look at them after 3 minutes, and thereafter keep a close eye on them until they begin to colour. Then remove them and cool them on a wire rack.

Mrs Perrot's Heart or Pound Cake

*A pound fine Sugar well dried & sifted a pd of new churn'd Butter beat into it
with a wooden slice, till they become an Oyl, in about ¹/₂ an hour, then add 8 eggs
very lightly beaten with half the whites, a tea cup mountain a nutmeg grated and a
small bit of Cinnamon sifted, keep all stirring till yᵉ oven is ready (which must be
made pretty hot, but yᵉ first heat let go a little off as they are apt to be over colour'd)
have ready a pd of flour well dried and no lumps as that makes em heavy, and mix
it with yᵉ rest just as its going into yᵉ oven If you chuse Currants ³/₄ of a pound
well washd & pick'd to be strew'd over them just as they are put into your Tins.*
(L.P., page 38.)

8 oz/225 g/1 cup softened, slightly salted butter

8 oz/225 g/1 ¼ cups caster (superfine) sugar

2 whole eggs and 2 yolks

8 oz/225 g/2 cups plain (all-purpose) flour

¹/₂ teaspoon salt

¹/₂ teaspoon grated nutmeg

pinch of ground cinnamon

175 g/6 oz/1 cup currants

4 tablespoons Malaga or Madeira wine (see below)

Our modern recipe is, in fact, for a 'half-pound' cake because 'a pound of
everything' would make a cumbersome offering for most occasions. The
'mountain' used by Mrs Perrot to moisten her cake was almost certainly
sweet Malaga but a medium-dry Madeira does equally well.

Grease and line an 8-inch/20-cm square cake tin (pan), and set the
oven to heat to 300°F/150°C/Gas Mark 2. Cream the butter and sugar
together until light and well blended. Add the whole eggs and yolks one
at a time, beating each in completely before adding the next. Separately
sift together the flour, salt and spices, then fold them into the creamed
mixture, beating to blend after each addition. Add the dried fruit in the
same way. Lastly stir in the liquor.

Turn the mixture into the tin, level the top and bake for 2 hours or
until the cake smells good and is golden and firm. Cool on a wire rack.

Entertaining Friends

A Nice Whet Before Dinner

Cut some slices of bread half an inch thick, fry them in butter, but not too hard, then split some anchovies, take out the bones, and lay half an anchovy on each piece of bread, have ready some Cheshire cheese grated, and some chopped parsley mixed together, lay it pretty thick over the bread and anchovy, baste it with butter and brown it with a salamander: it must be done on the dish in which you send it to table. (E.R. 1782, fac. 1970, page 139.)

SERVES 6

6 × 2 oz/50 g cans anchovy fillets in oil

a few tablespoons milk

16 thick slices from a large white tin loaf

extra good-quality olive oil

freshly grated Cheshire or Parmesan cheese

chopped parsley *or* strained orange or lemon juice

Professional chef William Verrall cut his whets into finger lengths, fried them in oil and strewed them with grated Parmesan cheese and orange or lemon juice: take your choice.

Drain the anchovies, reserving the oil, and soak the fillets in milk overnight. Next day, cut the crusts off the bread and toast the slices on one side until mid-brown, then turn them over and barely colour the second side. Cut each slice into 3 fingers, trimming any burned edges. Brush the barely toasted sides with the reserved anchovy oil; augment it with olive oil if needed.

Place 1 large or 2 small anchovy fillets on the oiled side of each toast finger, trimming off the pointed ends. Sprinkle generously with cheese, mixed with parsley if you are using it. Arrange the fingers, cheese side up, under a heated grill (broiler) and cook for just long enough to half-melt the cheese. If you are using fruit juice, sprinkle it over the fingers at this point. Then serve as soon as possible, very hot.

Summer Pease Soup

Take five or six Cucumbers pared and sliced the white part of as many Coss Lettice a sprig or two of Mint, two or three Onions, some pepper, a little salt a full pint of young Pease a little Parsley half a pound of butter put them altogether in a sauce pan to stew in their own liquor for an hour and half or till they are quite tender; then boil as many old Pease pulp them through a cullender and mix them in a quart of the liquor or more as you like it for thickness when the herbs are stewed enough put them in and serve it up. (M.L., page 6.)

SERVES 6

1 cucumber, about 14 oz/400 g weight, quartered lengthways

2 Cos (Romaine) lettuces or 1 head Chinese leaves

2 medium onions

5 oz/150 g/⅔ cup butter, chopped

2 sprigs mint

salt and pepper

8 oz/225 g/1 cup shelled fresh young peas

2 sprigs parsley

1 lb/450 g/2¼ cups large fresh marrowfat peas

Martha Lloyd recorded two recipes for Pease Soup. This one was obviously for summer use, since it contains cucumber, lettuces and parsley. The other, which used celery, anchovies and a thick mash of spinach and herbs, was probably for use later in the year.

Peel and slice the quartered cucumber. Cut off the roots of the lettuces or Chinese leaves if required, and take off the green outer leaves for a salad; slice the light-coloured inner part for the soup. Peel the onions and slice them thinly.

Put the sliced cucumber and shredded leaves in a stew-pan with half the butter. Add the mint leaves, onions, seasoning and young peas. Lastly chop and add the parsley, the rest of the butter and 3–4 tablespoons water. Cover the pan tightly and place over low heat. Cook gently, shaking the pan fairly often, until all the vegetables are soft.

While they are cooking, boil the marrowfat peas in plenty of lightly salted water until tender. Sieve them, or purée them in a food processor, with 1–1½ pints/575–850 ml/2½–3½ cups of their cooking liquid. The exact quantity will depend on how thick you want your soup. Combine the purée with the contents of the stew-pan, and mix them thoroughly before serving.

Onion Soup

Boil eight or ten large Spanish onions, in milk and water, change it three times, when they are quite soft, rub them through a hair sieve, cut an old cock in pieces, and boil it for gravy with one blade of mace, strain it, and pour it upon the pulp of the onions, boil it gently with the crumb of an old penny loaf, grated into half a pint of cream; add Chyan pepper and salt to your taste: a few heads of asparagus or stewed spinage, both make it eat well and look very pretty: grate a crust of brown bread round the edge of the dish. (E.R. 1792, fac. 1970, page 8.)

SERVES 6

about 2 lb/1 kg onions, peeled and sliced

1 ½ pints/850 ml/3 ⅔ cups milk and water mixed

1 blade mace

good pinch of grated nutmeg

salt and pepper to taste

1 ½ pints/850 ml/3 ⅔ cups chicken stock

6 fl oz/175 ml/¾ cup single (light) cream

2 oz/50 g/1 cup soft white breadcrumbs, made without crust

pinch of Cayenne pepper

about 3 oz/75 g/1 ½ cups dark brown (rye) breadcrumbs

about 24 cooked asparagus tips or a handful of young spinach leaves, blanched

This simple but dramatic creamy soup is well worth the trouble of using 3 pans.

Simmer the onions in the milk and water with the mace, nutmeg and seasoning for 10–15 minutes, until softened. Drain them. Put the chicken stock into a clean pan, add the onions and simmer again until they are fully cooked and very soft. While they cook, warm the cream and soak the white breadcrumbs in it.

Strain the stock into another pan. Either sieve the onions back into it, or process them in an electric blender, then add the pulp to the liquid. Sieve the crumb and cream mixture, or blend the crumbs and cream to a purée in an electric blender, then mix the purée into the soup. (If either the onions or the crumb mixture are stiff to handle in the blender, return a little of the soup mixture to the blender.) Season with salt and a pinch of Cayenne. Cook, without boiling, until very hot, then turn into well-heated individual soup bowls. Sprinkle the dark brown crumbs all around the edge of each bowl, and garnish the centre with asparagus tips or spinach leaves.

White Mushroom Fricassee

Take a quart of fresh mushrooms, make them very clean, cut the largest ones in two, put them in a stew-pan with four spoonfuls of water, a blade of mace, a piece of lemon-peel; cover your pan close, and stew them gently for half an hour, beat up the yolks of two eggs with half a pint of cream, and a little nutmeg grated in it, take out the mace and lemon-peel, put in the eggs and cream, keep it stirring one way all the time till it is thick, season with salt to your palate; squeeze a little lemon-juice in, butter the crust of a French roll and toast it brown; put it in your dish and the mushrooms over.

N.B. Be careful not to squeeze the lemon-juice in till they are finished and ready to put in your dish, then squeeze it in, and stir them about for a minute, then put them in your dish. (H.G. 1796, fac. 1971, page 229.)

SERVES 6

1 lb/450 g button mushrooms

2 fl oz/50 ml/¼ cup water

1 large piece of blade mace

1 strip lemon peel

2 egg yolks

1 tablespoon flour

good pinch of grated nutmeg

10 fl oz/275 ml/1¼ cups single (light) cream

salt and pepper

freshly made buttered toast

lemon juice if needed

Clean the mushrooms, trim them and cut off the stalks. Cut any large mushrooms in half. Put them in a pan with the water, mace and lemon peel, bring to simmering point, cover and cook very gently until the mushrooms are tender and the liquid is reduced almost to a glaze.

Mix one egg yolk with the flour to make a smooth paste, then blend in the remaining yolk, nutmeg, cream, and a little salt and pepper. Off the heat, remove the mace and lemon peel from the pan and stir in the egg/cream mixture. Replace over very low heat and stir continuously until the sauce thickens.

Lay the toast in a warmed serving dish ready to use. Taste the sauce and adjust the seasoning, adding a little lemon juice if needed. Spoon the mixture over the toast. Serve hot without delay.

Eggs and Onions, commonly called the Onion Dish

Boil some eggs hard; cut some onions in slices across, and fry them with brown'd butter; take them carefully out of the butter, and drain it from them; cut the eggs in round slices; beat some fresh butter; mix in some mustard and vinegar; then put in the eggs and onions, and toss it upon the fire, and dish it.
(S.McI. 1782, page 105.)

SERVES 1–2

3 hard-boiled eggs, briefly chilled

1 medium onion

salt and pepper

3 oz/75 g/6 tablespoons unsalted butter

1 teaspoon made English mustard

1 tablespoon white wine vinegar

As a lunchtime or late-night snack for 1 or 2 people, this slightly tart little dish will be a welcome alternative to A Pretty Dish of Eggs on page 93. It will be equally good as a garnish for roast beef.

Shell and slice the eggs, and discard any ends of white without yolk. Peel the onion, cut off the root and cut the flesh crossways into thin, round slices. Heat 1 oz/25 g/2 tablespoons of the butter in a frying-pan (skillet) and, when sizzling hot, add the onion slices. Fry over moderate heat until the butter begins to brown and the onion slices are tender; stir them all the time. Remove from the heat when done, and drain the onion on soft kitchen paper (paper towels).

Discard the browned butter, wipe the pan and put in the remaining 2 oz/50 g/4 tablespoons butter. Over gentle heat, mix in the mustard and vinegar. When the butter has melted, add the egg slices and onion, and toss them very gently until heated through. Serve on toast with a green side salad as a supper dish, or as a garnish for a winter meat or game dish.

Broil Eggs

Make a butterd Toast, break 7 eggs into boiling water, let them lay just to harden, put them on ye toast quite whole, grate a little nutmeg over them and squeeze lemon upon them, having your sallymander quite hot, hold it over them two or 3 minutes, till of quite a light brown. (L.P. from Lady Williams, page 55.)

SERVES 6

7 large slices bread from a tin loaf

butter

salt and pepper

a few drops white vinegar

7 small fresh eggs

grated nutmeg

lemon juice

Broiled eggs, like boiled ones, were probably served at both breakfast (for gentlemen) and at supper or a snack meal. This recipe can be interpreted in two ways. The eggs may have been cooked one by one and dressed on small squares or rounds of toast, or they may have been poached all together and treated as a grand single egg since the whites all mingled in the pan. This, although it creates a more dramatic dish, is tricky to serve, so I have used a variation of the first method.

Toast the bread on both sides but only lightly on the second side. Cut out the centre of each slice with a 3-inch/7.5-cm ring cutter. Butter the lightly toasted sides of the rounds. Arrange 6 in a circle on a warmed heatproof serving plate and put the seventh one in the centre; they should all touch their neighbours. Keep warm.

Put ½ inch/1 cm lightly salted water in a shallow pan, add the vinegar and bring to simmering point. Place the ring cutter in the water. Poach each egg in turn in the ring, putting half the white in first and letting it set before adding the remaining white and lastly the lightly seasoned yolk. As each egg is done, drain it in a perforated spoon, then place it on a round of toast. The eggs should be touching, so that when all are in place the dish looks like a posy of white daisies with yellow centres.

The illusion will be heightened by broiling the eggs. Sprinkle them lightly with grated nutmeg and a few drops of lemon juice and dot with butter. Place the plate of eggs on a grill (broiler) rack under medium heat and grill for 2 or 3 moments only, until lightly glazed. Serve as soon as possible, using a fish slice (spatula) to lift off the eggs and toasts individually.

Broiled Salmon

Cut fresh salmon into thick pieces, flour them and broil them, lay them in your
dish, and have plain melted butter in a cup; or anchovy and butter.
(H.G. 1796, fac. 1971, page 157.)

SERVES 6

6 salmon steaks, 1 inch/2.5 cm thick

salt and black pepper

flour for dusting

2 oz/50 g/4 tablespoons unsalted butter

extra melted butter to serve

Wipe the fish steaks with a damp cloth and season them with salt and
freshly ground black pepper. Dust them very lightly with flour on both
sides. Melt the butter in the bottom of a grill (broiler) pan, and turn the
steaks over in it to coat both sides with a film of fat. They should be about
3 inches/7.5 cm from the heat source. Cook the steaks for about 10
minutes under medium heat, basting with butter several times. Increase
the heat towards the end so that the tops of the steaks are lightly gilded.
Serve with extra melted butter in a sauce-boat.

Sole with Wine and Mushrooms

Skin, gut, and wash your soles very clean; cut off their heads, and dry your fish in a
cloth. Then very carefully cut the flesh from the bones and fins on both sides, and
cut the flesh long ways, and then across, so that each sole may be in eight pieces.
Take the heads and bones, and put them into a saucepan, with a pint of water, a
bundle of sweet herbs, an onion, a little whole pepper, two or three blades of mace,
a little salt, a small piece of lemon-peel, and a crust of bread. Cover it close, and
let it boil till half be wasted. Then strain it through a fine sieve, and put it into a
stewpan. Put in the soles, and with them half a pint of white wine, a little parsley
chopped fine, a few mushrooms cut small, a little grated nutmeg, and a piece of
butter rolled in flour. Set all together on the fire, but keep shaking the pan all the
while till the fish be enough. Then dish them up, and garnish with lemon.
(J.F. 7th edn, page 100.)

SERVES 4–6

2 lb/1 kg lemon sole fillets

heads, bones, skin and trimmings of fish

a bundle of sweet herbs (for example, tarragon or dill, marjoram, thyme, parsley)

1 medium onion, peeled and halved

4 black peppercorns

3 pieces of blade mace

1 strip lemon peel

1 crust stale bread

salt and pepper to taste

about 3 oz/75 g beurre manié made with 1½ oz/40 g each softened butter and flour

8 fl oz/225 ml/1 cup white wine

4 oz/110 g button mushrooms, quartered

a few drops of lemon juice

pinch of grated nutmeg

1 tablespoon chopped fresh parsley

lemon wedges

Each fish should yield 2 fillets, one from each side if small. Large fish may yield 2 fillets per side. Cut large fillets in half lengthways, and all fillets in half across. Then make a fish stock. Put the fish heads, bones, skin and trimmings into a pan with 1½ pints/850 ml/3¾ cups water, the herb bundle and onion. Add the peppercorns, mace and lemon peel tied in a muslin bag, and the bread crust. Season the stock to your taste, then cover the pan and cook until the contents are reduced to 15 fl oz/ 425 ml/just under 2 cups – half the original volume.

Strain the stock into a frying-pan (skillet) which will hold all the fish. Off the heat add 2 oz/50 g of the beurre manié in small portions and stir them in. Add the wine, mushrooms, lemon juice and nutmeg and stir round again. Place the pan over medium heat and simmer until the sauce is slightly thickened. Then add the fish fillets, and simmer again, shaking the pan gently, until they are cooked through. They should take only a few minutes.

With a perforated fish slice (spatula), lift the fish fillets and mushrooms into a warmed serving dish. If you wish, thicken the sauce a little more with the rest of the beurre manié. Pour some of the sauce over the fish and put the rest in a sauce-boat. Sprinkle the fish with the parsley and garnish it with lemon wedges before serving.

Mock Oyster Sauce

Take half a pint of Cream, one blade of Mace pounded or boiled with the Cream, thicken it with butter rolled in flour, & add essence of Anchovies to your taste, about one spoonful. (M.L., page 94.)

MAKES 10 FL OZ/275 ML/1¼ CUPS

1 oz/25 g/2 tablespoons slightly softened butter
flour for coating
10 fl oz/275 ml/1¼ cups single (light) cream
½–1 teaspoon ground mace
½–1 teaspoon Geo. Watkins Anchovy Sauce or anchovy essence

Form the butter into a sausage shape by rolling it around in a puddle of flour on a plate. Heat the cream almost to boiling point, sprinkling in the mace while doing so. Stir round to incorporate it.

Just before the cream reaches boiling point, take it off the heat and stir in the flour-coated butter in small bits; it should melt at once. Replace the saucepan over gentle heat and stir in the Anchovy Sauce. Simmer for a few moments to thicken slightly, then serve.

Butchers' Meats and Game

During the eighteenth century, as the Industrial Revolution got under way, the English became more and more renowned as heavy meat-eaters. Both pasture and livestock were being steadily improved, and the system of enclosures was concentrating land-holdings in fewer and fewer hands. The rich and middle rich, and professional people such as Parson Austen, could and did eat well, even though the last had only modest incomes.

The art of roasting meat was quite different from ours because joints were cooked on spits, turned constantly in front of a brisk fire. To prevent scorching, the meat was sometimes wrapped in oiled paper for most of its cooking time. Obviously meat cooked in that way cannot be compared with the modern oven-baking which we use as our 'roasting' technique now; and our broiling and stewing tools and techniques are likewise far removed from those of the past.

The table overleaf therefore shows modern roasting methods (quick and slow) for beef, veal, lamb and pork. There is also information below on venison and small, furred game. For interesting extra reading on Georgian meat cookery see *Food and Drink in Britain*, Chapter 3, by C. Anne Wilson (listed in the Bibliography).

Venison and Small, Furred Game

In Georgian England, venison and hares were reserved for 'qualified persons': that is, owners of parks and farmland, and their friends. Poachers were drastically punished, especially as the century progressed. For those who could get them, however, venison and hare were welcome luxuries.

Venison, then as now, needed hanging and marinating when brought in. It was hung in any cool, airy place free from flies for, say, 2–3 weeks before being jointed and marinated for 24–48 hours in red wine and oil with spices such as cloves, and root vegetables. Vinegar, ale and salt made an alternative 'drink'.

Haunch, shoulder and saddle were the main roasting joints of venison, as they are today. Chops, cutlets and fillet slices are still usually fried. Nowadays venison is often oiled and then roasted in foil or in a 'jacket' of flour paste to keep it moist until the coating is taken off to brown the meat surfaces. Roasting is best done at 375°F/190°C/Gas Mark 5, allowing 35 minutes per lb/450 g. Garnishing can and should be simple. The Georgians used a paste or jelly of barberries; redcurrant jelly is the obvious modern choice.

Hares and rabbits were also roasted in Georgian times. They can look splendid presented whole with head erect, but they are difficult to carve and are really better braised or jugged.

MODERN ROASTING TIMES

In all cases allow 5–10 minutes per lb/450 g extra for cooking stuffed joints.

	QUICK-ROAST	SLOW-ROAST	GRILL (BROIL)/FRY
Beef	*on the bone* 15 min. per lb/450 g + 15 min. *off the bone* 20 min. per lb/450 g + 20 min.	*on the bone* 20 min. per lb/450 g + 20 min. *off the bone* 30 min. per lb/450 g + 30 min.	*steaks* (*1 inch/2.5 cm thick*) rare 7 min. medium 10 min. well done 15 min.
Lamb	*on the bone* 20 min. per lb/450 g + 20 min. *off the bone* 25 min. per lb/450 g + 25 min.	*on the bone* 25 min. per lb/450 g + 25 min. *off the bone* 35 min. per lb/450 g + 35 min.	*chops* 12–15 min. *cutlets* 7–9 min.
Veal	*on the bone* 25 min. per lb/450 g + 25 min. *off the bone* 30 min. per lb/450 g	*on the bone* 35 min. per lb/450 g + 35 min. *off the bone* 40 min. per lb/450 g	*chops* 12–15 min.
Pork	*on the bone* 25 min. per lb/450 g + 25 min.	*off the bone* 35 min. per lb/450 g + 35 min.	*chops* 15–20 min.

Note: The times above are for a quick-roasting temperature of 425°F/220°C/Gas Mark 7. Slow-roasting of beef, lamb and veal should be done at a temperature of 350°F/180°C/Gas Mark 4. Slow-roasting of pork should be done at 375°F/190°C/Gas Mark 5.

Roast Ribs of Beef

*To roast a piece of beef about ten pounds will take an hour and a half, at a good
fire... Observe, in frosty weather your beef will take half an hour longer.
Be sure to paper the top, and baste it well all the time it is roasting, and throw
a handful of salt on it. When you see the smoak draw to the fire, it is near enough;
then take off the paper, baste it well, and drudge it with a little flour to make a fine
froth: take up your meat, and garnish your dish with nothing but horse-radish.
Never salt your roast meat before you lay it to the fire, for that draws out all the
gravy... (H.G. 1796, fac. 1971, page 16.)*

SERVES 6

5 ½ lb / 2.5 kg forerib of beef (standing rib roast)

2–3 oz / 50–75 g / ¼–⅓ cup clean beef dripping

2 tablespoons melted butter for 'frothing'

1 oz / 25 g / ¼ cup flour

pan-juice gravy (if serving hot)

Originally a joint like this one was spit-roasted. The technique is not
often practical today, but we *can* 'froth' our joint with butter and flour in
the old style after cooking it, to give it a rich colour.

Ask your butcher to trim the ends of the rib-bones so that the joint
stands level with both cut sides exposed to the heat. When ready to cook,
pre-heat the oven to 425°F/220°C/Gas Mark 7. Melt the dripping in a
roasting-tin (pan), stand the joint on a rack in the tin and brush the meat
with dripping. Roast it in the oven for 10 minutes. Then lower the heat to
350°F/180°C/Gas Mark 4. Cover the joint loosely with greaseproof
paper (or baking parchment) and roast for another 1½–1¾ hours for
under-done meat or for 2–2¼ hours for well-done meat. Baste the meat 2
or 3 times during cooking.

Fifteen minutes before you reckon the meat is done as you wish,
remove it from the oven, brush it with the melted butter and dredge it
with flour. Then return it to the oven to finish cooking.

Allow the meat to 'rest' for 15–20 minutes if you wish to serve it hot,
and meanwhile make gravy with the pan juices. For serving from a cold
side table or for a party or picnic meal, cool it under a cloth, then keep it
in a meat safe or cold larder until wanted.

In modern oven-roasting we can use a consistent high or low cooking
temperature: see the table opposite.

Fricandos of Veal

Take a leg of veal, and cut out of the thick part of it steaks half an inch thick, and six inches long. Lard them with small chardoons, and dredge them with flour. Broil them before the fire till they be of a fine brown, and then put them into a large tossing-pan, with a quart of good gravy, and let them stew half an hour. Then put in a slice of lemon, a little anchovy, two teaspoonfuls of lemon-pickle, a large spoonful of walnut catchup, the same of browning, a little chyan pepper, and a few morels and truffles. When your fricandos be tender, take them up, and thicken your gravy with butter and flour. Strain it, put your fricandos in the dish, pour your gravy upon them, and garnish with lemon and berberries. Some lay fried forcemeat balls round them, or forcemeat rolled in veal caul, and yolks of eggs boiled hard, which has a very good effect. (J.F. 7th edn, page 113.)

SERVES 6

6 slices veal, ½ inch/1 cm thick and weighing about 6 oz/150 g each
(veal or turkey escalopes can be used instead)

several sprigs fresh rosemary

salt and pepper

oil or butter for frying

2 pints/1.1 litres/5 cups chicken or veal stock

1 tablespoon lemon juice

1 tablespoon anchovy sauce or essence

2 or 3 tablespoons mushroom ketchup

4 oz/110 g mushrooms, finely chopped

Cayenne pepper

beurre manié made with 1 oz/25 g each softened butter and flour

Garnish

lemon wedges or slices

fresh stewed cranberries or cranberry sauce (see note below)

small forcemeat balls (see opposite)

1–2 hard-boiled egg yolks

Beat out the meat slices with a mallet or cutlet bat. Rub them over well with the rosemary and season to taste. Fry the meat in the oil or butter until just browned on each side, then transfer to a stew-pan and add the stock, lemon juice, anchovy sauce or essence, mushroom ketchup, the mushrooms and a pinch of Cayenne. Cook gently until tender.

Transfer the fricandos to a shallow serving dish and keep warm. Off the heat, add the beurre manié to the sauce in small spoonfuls, then reheat until it thickens to suit your taste. Pour the sauce over the fricandos and garnish the edge of the dish with lemon wedges or slices, cranberries and forcemeat balls. Crumble 1 or 2 hard-boiled egg yolks over the dish.

If possible, use fairly tart, fresh cranberries or sauce. A sickly-sweet sauce destroys the subtle mixture of flavours which makes this dish a sophisticated treat.

Forcemeat Balls

Take a little fat bacon, beat it in a marble mortar, take two anchovies, two or three pigeons' livers, chop them together; add a little lemon-peel shred, a little beaten mace, nutmeg, Cayenne, stale bread crumbs, and beef-suet an equal quantity, mix all together with an egg. (H.G. 1796, fac. 1971, page 119.)

MAKES 16 BALLS ABOUT 1 INCH/2.5 CM IN DIAMETER

4 oz/110 g/2 cups breadcrumbs

2 oz/50 g/scant ½ cup shredded suet

2 canned anchovy fillets, soaked, chopped and pounded

1 tablespoon chopped fresh parsley or ½ tablespoon dried oregano

grated rind of ½ lemon

salt and pepper

pinch each of grated nutmeg and ground mace

a few grains of Cayenne pepper

1 large egg, beaten

egg wash for glazing (optional)

The original mixture is stronger in flavour and fattier than we want for most purposes today, but you can add a finely chopped chicken liver and a chopped bacon rasher (slice) to the milder 'mix' here if you wish.

Mix together all the ingredients and adjust the quantity of breadcrumbs if required to make a mixture which will cohere when squeezed.

Roll into small balls, coat with egg wash and fry or bake until heated through.

Dressed Breast of Lamb

*Boil your breast of mutton till the bones will slip out, then take off skin & rub the
meat over with yolk of egg a few sweet herbs parsley onion, crumbs of bread with
salt and pepper chopp'd altogether and strewed over the meat, put it in a dutch oven
before a fire to brown dish it up with a rich gravy. (M.L., page 58.)*

SERVES 6–8

2 breasts of lamb (bone in)

1 egg yolk

3–4 tablespoons chopped mixed herbs (fresh if possible – try marjoram,
hyssop and tarragon)

1 tablespoon chopped fresh parsley

½ large onion, peeled and chopped

2 slices bread, crusts removed

salt and black pepper

about 25 g/1 oz/2 tablespoons butter, melted

watercress and lemon wedges to garnish (optional)

gravy (see page 42) or caper sauce (see page 102)

Lay the breasts, bone side up, in a stew-pan or pot-roaster with a lid and
add just enough water to cover. Boil gently for 40–50 minutes or until the
bone ends protrude and the rib-bones themselves slip out of the meat
easily. When cool enough to handle, take out the rib-bones and ease the
skin side of the spine loose from the flesh. It should then be fairly easy to
detach the spine, leaving two boneless, flat pieces of meat. Scrape or cut
off as much excess fat as you can, then rinse the breasts with boiling water
to detach the last loose fatty flakes. Mop dry with kitchen paper (paper
towels).

Lay the breasts side by side, boned side up, on a lightly greased
baking-tray. Brush the surfaces with egg yolk. Chop the herbs, parsley
and onion together. Do this in a food processor if you can, then tip out
the herb mixture on to soft kitchen paper and put the slices of crustless
bread and some seasoning into the machine: they will be processed in a
few seconds. Return the herb mixture and blend for a moment or two
more.

Heat the grill (broiler) while you spread the crumb mixture evenly
over the lamb breasts and sprinkle them with melted butter. (This is a
concession to modern taste; the Austens would have used melted mutton
fat.) Place the prepared tray of meat under the grill and cook until

lightly toasted on top. Serve, cut in pieces, on a large, flat platter with – a modern suggestion – a garnish of watercress and lemon wedges for squeezing. Offer gravy in a boat, or a caper sauce.

To Roast Geese, Turkies, &c.

When you roast a goose, turkey, or fowls of any sort, take care to singe them with a piece of white paper, and baste them with butter; dredge them with a little flour, and sprinkle a little salt on; and when the smoak begins to draw to the fire, and they look plump, baste them again, and dredge them with a little flour, and take them up.

As to geese and ducks, you should have sage and onion shred fine, with pepper and salt put into the belly, with gravy in the dish; or some like sage and onion and gravy mixed together. Put only pepper and salt into ... all ... sorts of wild fowl. A middling turkey will take an hour to roast; a very large one, an hour and a quarter; a small one, three quarters of an hour. You must paper the breast till it is near done enough, then take the paper off and froth it up. Your fire must be very good. The same time does for a goose. (H.G. 1796, fac. 1971, pages 20–1.)

Poultry

Most poultry is now sold ready-hung, plucked, drawn and trussed. Home-killed chickens, ducks and geese should be plucked while still warm and hung head downwards for 24–48 hours (depending on size) after being plucked and singed; today we singe off the down and hairs with a taper, not paper.

Remove the crop and windpipe at the neck end after taking off the head. Slit the vent wide open and pull out the innards and any excess fat with one hand. Cut the gall-bladder from the liver. Then slit the skin, but not the tendons, at each knee joint and pull out the leg tendons on the fleshy side by twisting a skewer round them. Put some chopped fresh herbs or a stuffing in the belly space.

Truss the bird so that it will keep its shape during cooking. Bard dry birds (chickens and guineafowl) with fat bacon. Prick the skins of ducks or geese to release some fat; only baste with fat, if you do it at all, during a bird's final browning.

Ignore Mrs Glasse's roasting times. Either she was an incurable optimist or her birds were a good deal smaller than ours. Follow the times and temperatures in any good standard cookbook.

Take the conventional tracklements for your dish from the same source. Duck demands green peas and apple sauce in summer, and goose squawks for sage and onion stuffing at Michaelmas and Christmas. Turkey was already a winter favourite in Jane's day too, especially for households with guests at Christmastide.

Game Birds

Small game birds may be split and grilled, but are more often roasted. They are brushed with melted butter or barded with fat bacon before being cooked, and the insides are moistened with a knob of seasoned butter. They are usually roasted on slices of toast and are served garnished with watercress and 'straw' potatoes.

Partridge seems to have been the most popular of the smaller birds in Cassandra's and Jane's circle, and it was probably served at home with Martha's Bread Sauce (page 86 of her MS), given her by Mr Hartley.

It reads: 'Put some bread Crums into a pan with a small Onion & a little Gravy, let it boil & then add a little Cream – take out the Onion before you put it into the boat & add a little salt to your taste.'

Pheasant à la Braise

Lay a layer of beef all over your pan, then a layer of veal, a little piece of bacon, a piece of carrot, an onion stuck with cloves, a blade or two of mace, a spoonful of pepper black and white, and a bundle of sweet herbs; then lay in the pheasant, lay a layer of veal and then a layer of beef to cover it, set it on the fire five or six minutes, then pour in two quarts of boiling gravy; cover it close and let it stew very softly an hour and a half, then take up your pheasant, keep it hot, and let the gravy boil till there is about a pint; then strain it off and put it in again, and put in a veal sweetbread, first being stewed with the pheasant; then put in some truffles and morels, some livers of fowls, artichoke-bottoms, and asparagus-tops (if you have them); let these simmer in the gravy about five or six minutes, then add two spoonfuls of catchup, two of red wine, and a little piece of butter rolled in flour, a spoonful of browning, shake all together, put in your pheasant, let them stew all together with a few mushrooms about five or six minutes more, then take up your pheasant and pour your ragoo all over, with a few force-meat balls. Garnish with lemon. You may lard it, if you choose. (H.G. 1796, fac. 1971, page 122.)

2–3 thin slices beef top rump

2–3 thin slices stewing veal

salt and mixed black and white pepper

1 fat pheasant (see note at end of method)

2–3 rashers (slices) fat bacon without rind

1 medium carrot, thickly sliced

1 onion, peeled and stuck with cloves

1 piece of blade mace

1 bouquet garni

1½ pints/850 ml/3⅔ cups chicken stock

forcemeat balls (see page 79)

1 egg yolk

8 oz/225 g prepared sweetbreads (calf's or lamb's)

1 × 20 g packet dried porcini mushrooms, soaked in water for 10–12 minutes and drained (optional)

2 tablespoons red wine plus extra if needed (see method)

butter for frying

8 oz/225 g chicken livers, cut in pieces

4 oz/110 g button mushrooms

beurre manié

lemon wedges or fans

This recipe is grander than any which the Austen family normally ate. It was most likely served as a first-course centre dish at a gentleman's dinner-party in his country mansion. For use today I have left out the artichoke bases and asparagus – but you can, of course, include them if you wish, simmered in lemon-flavoured water.

Arrange a layer of beef and veal so that it covers the bottom of a fairly large, flameproof casserole. Put a good seasoning of salt and pepper inside the pheasant. Then put the pheasant in the casserole, breast side up, and cover it with the bacon. Add the carrot and onion, mace and bouquet garni. Pour in the stock, cover the pan and cook gently for 45 minutes–1 hour, until the bird is tender. The time will depend on the bird's age and condition; an old bird may benefit by being turned over once or twice.

While the bird is cooking, make up the forcemeat. Form it into small balls, roll them in egg yolk slightly diluted with water and leave to firm up.

About 15 minutes before the end of the cooking time, add the sweet-breads to the stock, with the porcini if using them, and 2 tablespoons red wine. Fry the forcemeat balls in butter until lightly browned all over. Then fry the chicken livers and mushrooms in the same pan until tender. Keep these garnishing items warm under buttered paper.

Remove the bird from the casserole when cooked and keep it warm. Strain the sauce and add the sweetbreads to the other garnishings. (Discard the other meats.) Make up the sauce to 1¼ pints/700 ml/ 3 cups, using extra wine if needed. Stir in, by spoonfuls, enough beurre manié to thicken it as you wish. Taste, and adjust the seasoning.

To display the dish well, carve the bird at this stage. Then transfer the pieces to a carving dish and surround them with alternate clumps of the garnishings and with bright yellow lemon wedges or fluttery lemon fans. These garnishes make an epicure's dish out of an old or badly shot bird. Serve the sauce separately, in a well-heated sauce boat.

In other recipes Mrs Glasse recommends using a boiling fowl with or instead of a pheasant.

Jaune Mange

Steep two Oz. of Isinglass an Hour in a pint of Boiling water & if not dissolv'd in that time set it over the fire till it is; then strain it through a clean sive and let it stand a few minutes to settle. Then pour it into a Sauce pan & put near a pint of whitewine & the juice of two Oranges or one Lemon & the peel of one & the Yolks of eight eggs sweeten to your taste with Loaf Sugar, Set it over the fire, and keep it stirring till it just boils up & then strain it off into cups which must be wetted that they may turn out easily. (M.L., page 39.)

SERVES 6

2 tablespoons powdered gelatine

1 pint/575 ml/2½ cups hot water, in a saucepan

16 fl oz/450 ml/2 cups white wine

strained juice of 2 oranges

5 egg yolks, beaten

about 4 oz/110 g/⅔ cup caster (superfine) sugar

a few canned apricot halves and yellow blossoms to decorate

Scatter the gelatine little by little into the hot water in the saucepan and stir until it dissolves. Let it stand for a few moments to settle (there is no need to strain it). Then add the wine and orange juice, followed by the beaten egg yolks. Stir in the sugar a tablespoon at a time: try to judge how much you need by the strength and flavour of the wine, and blend it in thoroughly to make a smooth, sweet liquid.

Place the pan over low heat and bring the custard to simmering point very slowly. As soon as it begins to rise in the pan, strain it into a 2½-pint/1.4-litre/6¼-cup wetted mould or 6 individual moulds. Chill for 12–24 hours to firm up.

Turn out when firm and cold, and decorate with bits of canned apricot and small blossoms for a festive effect.

Solid Syllabubs

Mix a quart of thick raw cream, one pound of refined sugar, a pint and a half of fine raisin wine in a deep pan, put to it the grated peel and the juice of three lemons. Beat, or whisk it one way half an hour, then put it on a sieve with a bit of thin mustard laid smooth in the shallow end till next day. Put in glasses. It will keep good, in a cool place, ten days. (M.R. 1806 edn, page 204.)

SERVES 6

juice and grated rind of 1 lemon

1 tablespoon lump sugar, coarsely crushed

14 fl oz/400 ml/1¾ cups double (heavy) cream

7 oz/200 g/1 cup caster (superfine) sugar (see method)

8 fl oz/225 ml/1 cup medium-dry white wine

light sprinkling of dry English mustard powder (see method)

Put aside half the grated lemon rind and all lump sugar. Mix all the rest of the ingredients in a deep bowl. Use enough caster sugar to sweeten well but without being sickly; the exact quantity will depend on the sweetness of the wine. Use only a thin sprinkling of mustard; it should just give 'body' to the lemon and wine, not be noticable.

Beat the mixture in the bowl with an electric beater or rotary whisk until it is thick and stands in peaks. Turn it into sparklingly clean dessert glasses and chill overnight. As an attractive decoration, mix the reserved grated rind and crushed sugar and sprinkle this on the syllabubs just before serving.

Apple Puffs

Pare the fruit, and either stew them in a stone jar on a hot hearth, or bake them. When cold, mix the pulp of the apple with sugar and lemon-peel shred fine, taking as little of the apple-juice as you can. Bake them in thin paste in a quick oven; a quarter of an hour will do them if small. Orange or quince marmalade, is a great improvement. Cinnamon pounded, or orange-flower water in change.
(M.R. 1806, page 162.)

MAKES 8–10

12 oz–1 lb/350–450 g cooking (sharp) apples

1 teaspoon grated lemon rind

1 tablespoon fine-cut orange marmalade

soft brown sugar to taste

about 8 oz/225 g puff pastry (home-made or bought)

caster sugar for sprinkling

a little extra marmalade or Orange Peel 'Straws'
(see page 108)

Peel, core and slice the apples. Stew them in a very little water until tender. Drain well and reserve the cooking juice. Allow to cool completely. Then put the cooked apple pulp in a bowl and mix in the lemon rind and the marmalade. Taste and adjust the flavouring as required – add a little brown sugar, for instance.

Set the oven to heat to 425°F/220°C/Gas Mark 7. Grease and flour a baking-sheet lightly or cover with baking parchment. Roll out the pastry and cut it into 4-inch/10-cm squares. Divide the apple purée between them, placing it in a line across the centre of each square and stopping well short of the ends. Dampen the edges of the pastry and fold the two edges parallel with the line of filling over the purée. Pinch and seal these edges together, forming a tube. Then pinch the ends of each tube together, to seal them. Brush the pastry lightly with the reserved apple juice and sprinkle with caster sugar. Bake the puffs on the baking-sheet for about 20 minutes. Serve warm, topped with a little extra marmalade or Orange Peel 'Straws'.

Naples Biskets

Take 3 Egs both Yolkes & Whites, & beat them in a bason, or wooden Bowle a quarter of an hour, then put to them halfe a pound of Sugar, & beat them together as longe againe, then put to them 6 Ounces of fine flower & a graine or 2 of muske, being Steeped in a Spoonfull or two of Rosewater, & beat them well together while your Oven is a heating, & when it is as hot as for Manchett, butter your pans, & put your bread into them & backe it, & dry it, & keep it for your Use.
(D.R. 1698, fac. 1968, page 9.)

MAKES 30–36

3 eggs

8 oz/225 g/1 ¼ cups caster (superfine) sugar

2 teaspoons rose-water

2–3 drops rose flavouring

6 oz/175 g/1 ½ cups plain (all-purpose) flour

butter for greasing

Pre-heat the oven to 375°F/190°C/Gas Mark 5. Whisk the eggs until blended and frothy. Continue whisking, adding the sugar gradually, until the mixture is very thick and pale. Add the rose-water and flavouring, then sift in the flour while whisking. Grease sponge finger tins (pans) with a film of butter. Then, using 2 small spoons, fill the tins three-quarters full. Bake in the oven for 8–10 minutes, or until firm and light fawn. Lower the heat to 300°F/150°C/Gas Mark 2 and bake for another 5 minutes if you want them well dried. Cool on a wire rack.

Naples biscuits were originally made to be stored for serving when needed. They were used to make many sweet dishes and to accompany others. A simpler expedient was to slice tea cakes and dry them in the oven like rusks. Instead you could cut up fingers of bought plain slab Madeira cake and toast them until browned on both sides. These toasted fingers will stay soft in the middle.

A Fine Cake

Take a pound of fine flour dried & sifted, a pound of butter rubing it into the flour, take 3 pound of currants wash'd & pick'd, and set in an oven to dry, then mix them in the flour after the butter, then take candid orrange peel lemon, sittron & Apricot of each a quarter of a pound, a Nutmeg, & some mace, mix them together & four eggs but two whites, beat the eggs well with two spoonfuls of sack, & a pint of Yeast, & a pint of cream, boild & let stand to be cold, then strain them & make it into an indifferent stiff paste, keep out some of the cream till you see how it is; let it stand an hour before the fire to rise, & when the oven is hot turn it into a hoop & work it with your hands, let the hoop be butter'd. Dont rub the butter to hard in the flour. (M.L., page 27.)

8 oz/225 g/1 cup butter

8 oz/225 g/1¼ cups caster (superfine) sugar

4 eggs, separated

1 lb/450 g/4 cups plain (all-purpose) flour, sifted

¼ teaspoon grated nutmeg

pinch of ground mace

1½ lb/700 g/4½ cups mixed dried fruit

6 oz/175 g/1 cup cut mixed candied peel

1 oz/25 g compressed fresh yeast

about 5 fl oz/150 ml/⅔ cup milk to mix

Cream the butter and sugar in a mixing bowl. Beat in the egg yolks. Mix together the flour, nutmeg and mace, and add them to the butter-sugar mixture in small portions. Then beat in the dried fruit and peel, again in small portions, to prevent lumps forming in the dough.

In a smaller bowl, cream the yeast with a little of the milk and add it to the cake mixture. Then add enough extra milk to make a stiff paste. Beat the egg whites until frothy and blend them into the mixture. Cover the bowl and let it stand in a warm place for 1 hour to rise.

Heat the oven to 325°F/170°C/Gas Mark 3; grease and line a 9-inch/23-cm round loose-based cake tin (pan). Work the cake mixture with your hands to make a stiff paste. Turn it into the tin and bake in the oven for 2½ hours, or until a skewer pushed into the centre comes out dry. During baking, cover the top of the cake with baking parchment if it seems to be darkening too much.

If you wish to ice the cake in Regency style, see page 122.

Picnics and Visits

A picnic at Longleat, 1816, as depicted by Humphry Repton.

Broccoli, Hot or Cold

Strip all the little branches off till you come to the top one, then with a knife peel off all the hard outside skin, which is on the stalks and little branches, and throw them into water. Have a stew-pan of water with some salt in it; when it boils put in the broccoli, and when the stalks are tender it is enough, then send it to table with a piece of toasted bread soaked in the water the broccoli is boiled in under it, the same way as asparagus, with butter in a cup. The French eat oil and vinegar with it.

BROCCOLI AS A SALAD

Broccoli is a pretty dish by way of salad in the middle of a table; boil it like asparagus . . .; lay it in your dish, beat up with oil and vinegar and a little salt. Garnish with nastertium-buds. (H.G. 1796, fac. 1971, pages 30 and 231.)

SERVES 6

3 lb / 1.4 kg broccoli

salt

To Serve Hot

freshly ground black pepper

melted butter

To Serve Cold

oil

vinegar

pickled nasturtium buds or capers to garnish

nasturtium flowers (optional)

Use green Calabrese broccoli if possible, since it stores and freezes well. Buy 8 oz / 225 g per person to allow for leaf and stem wastage.

Divide the broccoli heads into small pieces or sprigs. Scrape the central stalks if tender, and cut into small pieces; discard them and any other stems if tough. Wash the broccoli you will use.

Bring a pan of salted water to the boil and put in the broccoli. Boil for 15 minutes or until tender.

To serve hot, drain and turn into a warmed serving dish. Season with freshly ground black pepper, and spoon melted butter over the sprigs. Serve extra melted butter in a sauce-boat.

To serve cold, drain the cooked broccoli well, then season lightly with oil and vinegar. Add nasturtium buds or capers and decorate with nasturtium flowers if you can.

Salmagundy

Is a beautiful small dish, if in nice shape, and if the colours of the ingredients are varied. For this purpose chop separately the white part of cold chicken or veal, yolks of eggs boiled hard, the white of eggs; parsley, half a dozen anchovies, beet-root, red pickled cabbage, ham, and grated tongue, or anything well-flavoured, and of a good colour. Some people like a small proportion of onion, but it may be better omitted.

A saucer, large tea-cup, or any other base, must be put into a small dish; then make rows round it wide at bottom, and growing smaller towards the top; choosing such of the ingredients for each row as will most vary the colours. At the top a little sprig of curled parsley may be stuck in; or, without any thing on the dish, the salmagundy may be laid in rows, or put into the half-whites of eggs, which may be made to stand upright by cutting off a bit at the round end. In the latter case, each half-egg has but one ingredient. Curled butter and parsley may be put as garnish between. (M.R. 1806 edn, page 205.)

Most ingredients for this colourful party dish have not changed at all since eighteenth-century cooks first made it, so you can choose how to arrange them to suit yourself and the number of people you have to feed. If you can, arrange them in circles on an inverted bowl, as Mrs Rundell did, and make them stick to it with softened butter. But if you are short of time or have a buffet party, you will probably find it easier to arrange them in rows, placing the green, red and yellow ingredients alternately. Another way is to put the main ingredients in alternately coloured, separate clumps on a bed of watercress or shredded lettuce leaves, laid on a tray. If you want to transform them into stuffed eggs, remember to chop the filling ingredients finely.

For a picnic party, put the fillings into separate cartons, and supply plastic spoons and forks for handling them. All the ingredients can be bought at any good supermarket or delicatessen.

* White meat of chicken or turkey, chopped.
* Hard-boiled eggs: at least 1 per person and several extras (even the most carefully boiled egg yolks can turn out grey). Always try to use unchilled eggs; crack and cool them quickly after boiling, then quarter or chop the yolks as soon as they are quite cold. Season both whites and yolks well and sprinkle with chopped parsley.
* Anchovy fillets canned in olive oil. There are usually 8 fillets in a 2 oz/50 g can. Drain and soak in milk overnight, then use whole or snip across into small bits. Alternatively serve soused or other pickled herrings (see Jemeca 'Trouts', page 103).
* Pickled or plain cooked beetroot, whole or shredded, usually sold in jars or vacuum packs. Plain cooked beetroot need seasoning.

* Pickled red cabbage, sold shredded in jars.
* Cooked ham and tongue cut in small strips.
* Any bright- or dark-coloured salad and herb leaves, de-stalked and shredded if large.
* Cucumbers and/or celery cut small (a suggestion from Mrs Glasse).
* Pickles of your choice, home-made or bought, including capers and lemon slices (sold in jars).
* Butter curls or balls as a garnish. Oil and vinegar as a dressing.

Oysters, Stewed and in Loaves

TO STEW OYSTERS

Open and separate the liquor from them, then wash them from the grit; strain the liquor, and put with the oysters a bit of mace and lemonpeel, and a few white peppers. Simmer them very gently, and put some cream and a little flour and butter. Serve with sippets.

OYSTER LOAVES

Open them, and save the liquor; wash them in it; then strain it through a sieve, and put a little of it in a tosser with a bit of butter and flour, white pepper, a scrape of nutmeg, and a little cream. Stew them, and cut in dice; put them into rolls sold for the purpose. (M.R. 1806 edn, page 22.)

SERVES 1 OR MORE

6 or more fresh oysters

1 piece of blade mace, 1 strip lemon peel and 4 white peppercorns or
a good pinch each of grated nutmeg and white pepper

small vol-au-vent cases or small rolls to serve

For each 2 oysters

2 teaspoons butter

2 teaspoons flour

1 tablespoon single (light) cream

2 tablespoons oyster liquor

Steam the oysters in a covered frying-pan (skillet) with as little water in it as possible, so that it does not get into the shells when they open. Alternatively put them, flat side down, on a ceramic plate and place it in a microwave for about 2 minutes (the liquor may spill out on to the plate).

As soon as they open, lift them out carefully with a slotted spoon and leave them to cool.

When they are cool enough to handle, strain off the liquor into a small bowl and add 1 piece of blade mace, 1 strip lemon peel and 4 white peppercorns for each 6 oysters. Infuse for 5–10 minutes. (Substitute a pinch each of grated nutmeg and ground white pepper if you are going to serve the oysters in 'loaves' – that is, in rolls.) Then for each 2 oysters stir together in a small pan 2 teaspoons each of butter and flour, 1 tablespoon single cream and 2 tablespoons oyster liquor (include a little more cream if needed). Quarter the oysters, and simmer them in the sauce until the edges curl. Serve in vol-au-vent cases or small rolls. Serve warm if possible.

A Pretty Dish of Eggs

Boil six eggs hard, peel them, and cut them into thin slices, put a quarter of a pound of butter into the stew-pan, then put in your eggs and fry them quick: half a quarter of an hour will do them. You must be very careful not to break them; throw over them pepper, salt, and nutmeg, lay them in your dish before the fire, pour out all the fat, shake in a little flour, and have ready two shalots cut small; throw them into the pan, pour in a quarter of a pint of white wine, a little juice of lemon, and a little piece of butter rolled in flour, stir all together till it is thick; if you have not sauce enough, put in a little more wine, toast some thin slices of bread cut three-corner ways, and lay round your dish, pour the sauce all over, and send it to table hot. You may put sweet oil on the toast, if it be agreeable.
(H.G. 1796, fac. 1971, page 234.)

SERVES 4–6

6 square slices freshly-made toast, without crusts

12 or more cold hard-boiled eggs

unsalted butter for frying

salt and freshly ground black pepper

good pinch of grated nutmeg

Sauce

1 tablespoon melted unsalted butter

2 shallots or 1 small onion, peeled and chopped

1 tablespoon plain (all-purpose) flour

salt and pepper

6 fl oz/175 ml/¾ cup medium-dry white wine

93

Modern city-bought eggs are so unreliable as to age, and design when cut, that you will be wise to hard-boil several extras to allow for ones with yolks right at one end. You want circles of yolk in the centre of white circles.

Make the toast first and keep warm. Shell enough eggs to provide 24–30 presentable, round slices ¼ inch/5 mm thick. Coat the base of a large frying-pan (skillet) with melted butter. With a palette knife (spatula), put in enough egg slices to cover the base side by side. Shake the pan gently over low heat for 2–3 minutes, turning the slices over once; they brown very quickly. When they have browned on both sides, transfer the slices to soft kitchen paper (paper towels); continue frying until all are browned, adding more butter as required.

Keep aside the 6 best slices for garnishing and pile the rest on a warmed serving platter, leaving room for the toast round the edge. Sprinkle with salt, pepper and nutmeg, then keep warm while completing the dish.

Put 1 tablespoon melted butter into a saucepan and add the shallots or onion. Stir over medium heat until they soften. Off the heat, blend in the flour and season well. Then stir in the wine gradually, with a little more butter from the frying-pan if you wish. Replace the sauce over low heat and stir until the mixture thickens. Leave at the side of the stove.

Cut each slice of toast into 2 triangles. Arrange on the edge of the dish with the longest point outwards. Pour the sauce over the eggs and part of the toast, leaving the outer points exposed. Arrange the reserved egg slices on top of the sauce.

Wine-roasted Gammon

*Take off the swerd, or what we call the skin, or rind, and lay it in lukewarm water
for two or three hours; then lay it in a pan, pour upon it a quart of canary, and let
it steep in it for ten or twelve hours. When you have spitted it, put some sheets of
white paper over the fat side, pour the canary in which it was soaked in the
dripping-pan, and baste it all the time it is roasting; when it is roasted enough pull
off the paper, and dredge it well with crumbled bread and parsley shred fine; make
the fire brisk, and brown it well. If you eat it hot, garnish it with raspings of bread:
if cold, serve it on a clean napkin, and garnish it with parsley for a second course.*
(H.G. 1796, fac. 1971, page 86.)

SERVES 6

1 unsmoked gammon joint, weighing about 4½ lb/2 kg

1 bottle medium-dry white wine

melted butter for coating

3 oz/75 g/¾ cup dried breadcrumbs

2 tablespoons chopped fresh parsley

Weigh the joint, then soak it in cold water for several hours or overnight.
Drain it, put it into a fair-sized pan and cover it with the wine. Bring it
gently to simmering point and simmer it for 12 minutes per lb/450 g plus
12 minutes more.

Remove the meat from the pan, pat it dry with kitchen paper (paper
towels) and let it cool a bit. Pre-heat the oven to 350°F/180°C/Gas
Mark 4. Lay the meat on a rack in a roasting-tin (pan), pour the cooking
liquid back over it and cover it closely with well-buttered greaseproof
paper (baking parchment). Roast it in the oven for 10 minutes
per lb/450 g, basting it often with the liquid.

When the meat is done, lay it on a board, take off any strings and strip
off the skin. Retie if required. Brush the meat lightly with the melted
butter. Mix together the breadcrumbs and chopped parsley and press
the mixture all over the fatty side of the meat to coat it. Raise the oven
temperature to 400°F/200°C/Gas Mark 6 and return the joint to the
oven for 10 minutes to let the coating brown lightly.

You can serve the joint hot if you wish, but it was and is more often served
cold; it was a feature, for instance, of the cold buffet served at the
Vauxhall Pleasure Gardens in London and was a popular second-course
dish at dinner-parties.

Veal or Venison 'Cake'

Bone a fat breast of Veal, cut some slices of Ham, the Yolks of six Eggs boiled hard & a handful of parsley chopped fine; cut your Veal into three pieces, put the fat piece at the bottom of a Cake Tin, then season it with pepper salt & the parsley Eggs & Ham between each layer, put the thinnest piece of Veal at the Top, & a Coffee cup of Water over it Bake it three Hours in a quick Oven with the bones over it – When done take them off & lay a weight on your meat in a small plate – as it cools the weight must be heavier that the Cake may be close & firm – The Brisket of the Veal is the only part used. (M.L., page 87.)

SERVES 6

2 ½ lb/1.1 kg lean veal or venison, boned (keep the bones)

salt and pepper

8 hard-boiled egg yolks

8 large sprigs parsley, chopped

1 lb/450 g rindless streaky bacon rashers (slices)

10 fl oz/275 ml/1 ¼ cups meat stock

The original recipe uses a fat breast of veal boned by the cook. It is baked in 3 layers sandwiched with ham, hard-boiled egg yolks and parsley. For a cooked cold dish to feed 6, a piece of meat weighing at least 2 ½ lb/1.1 kg is needed plus about 18 oz/500 g filling. The type of meat and the cut you use are less important than to have a joint which will provide three equal-sized layers of meat for an 8 × 4 inch/20 × 10 cm loaf-shaped baking-tin (pan). Thus, if veal is hard to get, you can use 2 breasts of lamb or 1 large boned shoulder, or a boned breast of young venison.

Cut the meat into 3 equal-sized slices, to fit your tin. Lay the thickest slice in the tin and season lightly. Crumble 4 of the egg yolks and mix with 4 tablespoons of the parsley. Spread the mixture over the meat. Cut the bacon rashers in half lengthways and arrange half the strips in a layer over the egg mixture. Cover with a second meat layer and reseason. Repeat the egg layer, cover with the remaining bacon and complete the dish with the third meat layer. Season again.

Pre-heat the oven to 325°F/170°C/Gas Mark 3. Add the stock to the tin. Cover the meat with the bones and then with a sheet of baking parchment, followed by one of foil. Bake the 'cake' for 3 hours.

When the meat is done, remove the coverings and bones, and pour off any excess stock. Cover with a weight and leave to cool overnight. Turn out to serve, and slice with a sharp knife. If you wish, you can brush the 'cake' with glaze (see page 42) before slicing.

Pigeon Pie

Rub the pigeons with pepper and salt, inside and out; in the former put a bit of butter, and if approved, some parsley chopped with the livers, and a little of the same seasoning, Lay a beef steak at the bottom of the dish, and the birds on it; between every two a hard egg. Put a cup of water in the dish; and if you have any ham in the house, lay a bit on each pigeon: it is a great improvement to the flavour. Observe when ham is cut for gravy or pies, to take the under part rather than the prime.

Season the gizzards, and the two joints of the wings, and put them in the centre of the pie; and over them in a hole made in the crust, three feet nicely cleaned to show what pie it is. (M.R. 1806 edn, page 134.)

SERVES 6

12 oz/350 g puff pastry

6 pigeons, plucked and gutted

salt and pepper

1 large carrot, thickly sliced

1 large onion, peeled and roughly chopped

spice bundle (a few black peppercorns, allspice and juniper berries, and 2 cloves, tied in a bit of muslin)

4 shallots, peeled and chopped

4 oz/110 g button mushrooms, quartered

2 oz/50 g/4 tablespoons unsalted butter

6 oz/175 g sliced cooked ham or gammon, cut into small strips

8 oz/225 g good steak, beaten and cut into small thin slices

seasoned flour for sprinkling

4 hard-boiled egg yolks, quartered

egg wash for glazing

Cold pigeon pies were popular fare for summer picnics, and indeed still are; only today we use the pinions and other oddments for gravy to moisten the meat instead of using them for show.

Roll out the pastry to fit an inverted 1¾-pint/1-litre/4½-cup English pie dish with 1½ inches/4 cm to spare all round. Leave to rest for 30 minutes.

Carefully separate the pigeon breasts from the carcases. Season the carcases and put them into a fairly large pan with the carrot, onion and spice bundle. Cover with water. Simmer for about 40 minutes, then strain the stock into a bowl and discard the bones, vegetables and spices.

Meanwhile sauté the shallots and mushrooms in about 1 oz/25 g/ 2 tablespoons of the butter until both are softened; use more butter if you need it. Add the ham or gammon. Sprinkle the steak with seasoned flour, then layer the steak, quartered hard-boiled egg yolks, shallots, mushrooms, ham and pigeon breasts in the pie dish with a pie funnel in the centre. Fill up the dish with the stock and leave to cool.

Pre-heat the oven to 425°F/220°C/Gas Mark 7. Cut off a 1-inch/ 2.5-cm strip around the edge of the pastry. Moisten the rim of the pie dish and fit on the strip, sealing the join. Moisten the strip lightly and fit on the pastry cover. Knock up or flute the edge if you wish. Cut some triangular slits in the crust to let steam escape, lift the flaps slightly, then brush the crust with egg wash.

Bake the pie for 15 minutes, then reduce the heat to 350°F/180°C/Gas Mark 4 and cook for about 1 1/2 hours longer. Cover the pie with wetted greaseproof paper (or baking parchment) half-way through to prevent the pastry over-browning and hardening.

If you want jellied stock for a cold picnic pie, add 1 good teaspoon soaked powdered gelatine to the stock when making it.

Chicken Baskets

Take one pound of the inside of a cold loin of veal, or the same quantity of cold fowl, that have been either boiled or roasted, a quarter of a pound of beef-suet, chop them as small as possible, with six or eight sprigs of parsley, season them well with half a nutmeg grated fine, pepper and salt, put them in a tossing-pan with half a pint of veal gravy, thicken the gravy with a little flour and butter, and two spoonfuls of cream, and shake them over the fire two minutes, and fill your patties. You must make your patties thus: raise them of an oval form, and bake them as for custards, cut some long narrow bits of paste and bake them on a dusting box, but not to go round, they are for handles; fill your patties when quite hot with the meat, then set your handles a-cross the patties; they will look like baskets if you have nicely pinched the walls of the patties, when you raised them; five will be a dish: you may make them with sugar and currants instead of parsley.
(H.G. 1796, fac. 1971, page 204.)

MAKES 8

14 oz/400 g shortcrust pastry

Filling

1 lb/450 g cooked chicken without skin or bones

2 oz/50 g/scant ½ cup shredded suet

1 large slice white bread without crust, crumbled

1 tablespoon chopped fresh parsley

½ teaspoon grated lemon rind

pinch of grated nutmeg

salt and white pepper

1 oz/25 g/2 tablespoons softened butter

1 oz/25 g/¼ cup flour

10 fl oz/275 ml/1¼ cups chicken stock

1 tablespoon double (heavy) cream

These little 'baskets' are attractive for a party, but hooped 'handles' are quite tricky to make; so for everyday or picnic use, simply lay a straight strip of pastry across the centre of each basket just before serving.

Pre-heat the oven to 375–400°F/190–200°C/Gas Mark 5–6. Round pastry cases are usually easier to make than oval ones, so I have used deep bun tins (muffin pans) for this recipe. Roll out the pastry and use it to line 8 tins each 3 inches/7.5 cm in diameter and 1 inch/2.5 cm deep. Pinch the top edge of each pastry case (shell) into a decorative pattern.

For the handles, cut out 8 strips of pastry each 3½ inches/9 cm long. Lay them side by side on a baking-sheet. (For hooped handles, bend them into semi-circular shapes with the ends almost as wide apart as the diameter of the baskets. Make a few extra handles in case of breakages.)

Bake the cases and handles 'blind' until fully cooked. The cases should take 8–10 minutes plus 3–4 minutes after removing the 'blind' filling. The handles should take only 5–6 minutes. Keep aside.

To prepare the filling, mince (grind) together the chicken meat, suet, crumbled bread, parsley, lemon rind, nutmeg and seasoning. Blend the butter and flour together with a little stock to make a soft paste. Bring the remaining stock almost to boiling point, then drop in the butter-flour paste in small spoonfuls and simmer, stirring, until the sauce is very thick. Add the chicken mixture and heat through, still stirring.

To serve the baskets hot, cover the filling and keep it warm while warming the pastry cases gently in the oven. Arrange the cases on a dish, fill them with chicken mixture and span each case with a pastry handle. For serving cold, cool the filling before putting it into the cold cases, and top with tiny sprigs of parsley before inserting the handles.

Martha's Gingerbread 'Cakes'

Take four Pints of flour rub into it 3 quarters of a pd. of butter 2 oz: of Ginger a Nutmeg, one oz: of Carraway seeds a quarter of a pint of Brandy 2 pd. of treacle, mix it altogether; & let it lay till it grows stiff then roll it out, & cut it into cakes, you may add what sweetmeats you please. (M.L., page 17.)

MAKES 14

7 oz/200 g/1 ¾ cups plain (all-purpose) flour, plus extra for dusting

½ tablespoon ground ginger

½ tablespoon grated nutmeg

2 oz/50 g/4 tablespoons butter

1 teaspoon caraway seeds (optional)

4 oz/110 g/⅓ cup black treacle (molasses; see note at end of method)

1 generous tablespoon brandy

flaked almonds

Sift together the flour, ginger and nutmeg into a bowl. Rub in the butter until the mixture is like crumbs. Add the seeds, if you are using them. Set the oven to heat to 350°F/180°C/Gas Mark 4 and put the opened treacle tin in the oven to warm. As soon as the treacle is liquid, pour 4 fl oz/110 g/⅓ cup into a measuring jug and stir in the brandy; keep stirring until it is blended in.

Slowly blend the warmed treacle mixture into the spiced flour. It will make a soft, sticky dough. Turn it on to a flat plate and leave it in a cool place until firm. (Chill it if you like, but you may have trouble dislodging it from the plate.)

Dust a work surface or board lightly with flour. Roll out the dough not less than ¼ inch/5 mm thick and cut it into rounds with a 2-inch/5-cm round cutter. If the dough is difficult to cut neatly, roll the rough pieces into balls with your palms and press lightly to flatten. Arrange the biscuits (cookies) on baking parchment on a baking-sheet and top each with an almond flake. Bake for 10 minutes. Cool on the sheet until quite cold, then store in an airtight tin.

You may find the mixture easier to manage if you use half black treacle and half golden syrup.

Stillroom Crafts

Few of us today are as practised as Mrs Austen and her daughters in the crafts of pickling and jamming, preserving and making wines and cordials. So it is a good thing that many of the preserves they used to make are now prepared by commercial firms of good repute, in some cases rather better than we can make them at home: sauces and pickles, in particular, both the traditionally English and the foreign ones such as soy sauce and piccalilli. In my own larder are sauerkraut and pickled red cabbage, cucumbers and lemon slices, walnuts, redcurrant jelly (instead of Jane Austen's pickled barberries), several jams, and whole-fruit preserves such as candied fruits.

The Austen ladies' marmalades were somewhat different from ours. Originally a marmalade had been a stiff quince-and-sugar paste from Portugal, but apricots and many other fruits had been used for it since Tudor times. Oddly, even in the eighteenth century some cooks still seemed to have no very clear notion of how to make a 'marmalett'. In the early part of the century one lady called Rebecca Price used pale, barely ripe apricots. Restaurateur John Farley, later in the same century, used over-ripe apricots not good enough for candying. Orange marmalade sometimes, but not always, included slivers of peel.

Some crushed fruit mixtures simply boiled to a soft mass with sugar syrup began to be called jam soon after 1700, when used for tart fillings and spreads. The term was familiar to both Cassandra and Jane. But there was still some confusion. In 1829 the writer Meg Dods published a recipe for 'Apricot and Plum Jam or Marmalade', treating them as the same product.

The processes of making pickles and sweet preserves have not changed much since Jane's time, although many more varieties were made then than today, and you may have to hunt for some ingredients such as whole spices and unusual vegetables in Asian or health-food stores. For making country home-made wines or cordials, you will also need some equipment from a specialist supplier.

Dr Kitchiner's Caper Sauce

To make a Quarter of a Pint, take a tablespoon of Capers, and two tea-spoonsful of Vinegar.
The present fashion of cutting Capers *is to mince one-third of them very fine, and divide the others in half; put them into a quarter of a pint of melted Butter, or good thickened Gravy; stir them the same way as you did the melted butter, or it will oil.*
Obs.—*Some boil and mince fine a few leaves of Parsley, or Chervil, or Tarragon, and add these to the sauce;—others the juice of half a Seville Orange, or Lemon.*
Mem.—*Keep the Caper bottle very closely corked, and do not use any of the Caper liquor:—if the Capers are not well covered with it, they will immediately spoil; and it is an excellent ingredient in Hashes, &c. The Dutch use it as a Fish Sauce, mixing it with melted butter. (W.K. 1836, page 229.)*

MAKES ABOUT 5 FL OZ/150 ML/⅔ CUP

1 tablespoon capers

2 teaspoons white wine vinegar

½ teaspoon finely chopped fresh parsley leaves

Melted butter

2 oz/50 g/4 tablespoons butter

2 heaped teaspoons flour

2 tablespoons whole milk

5 tablespoons water

Dr Kitchiner's recipe seems confusing at first sight. Its main ingredients are imported capers bottled in a liquid (the caper liquor) and the 'melted butter' which was a forerunner of white sauce.

Chop one-third of the capers into small bits and halve the rest if large. Put them all in a small bowl with the vinegar and parsley leaves. Keep aside while you make the 'melted butter'. For this, chop the butter and put it in a small saucepan with the flour and milk. Stir vigorously over gentle heat until melted and blended, then stir in the water and bring to the boil. Allow to cool somewhat, then blend in the capers, vinegar and parsley. Use at once or refrigerate in a jar with a tight, vinegar-proof lid for up to 48 hours.

Curree Powder

Take of Termeric Root, & Galangal Root each half an oz. Best Cayenne Pepper a quarter of an oz. Let the Termeric & Galangal be reduced to a fine powder separately, then mix them with the other articles & keep for use – NB. two oz. of Rice powderd to be mixed also with the other ingredients. – Mrs. Jane Fowle.
(M.L., page 76.)

MAKES ABOUT 3½ OZ/95 G

½ oz/15 g ground galangal

½ oz/15 g ground turmeric

¼–½ teaspoon cayenne pepper, or to taste

2 oz/50 g/½ cup rice flour

Turmeric (as we spell it) can be bought ready-ground in most supermarkets, but for the fresh root one must go to a city Asian fresh-food shop. Galangal or galanga root is also sold fresh or dried in Thai and other Asian stores; for some recipes you can use scrapings of the fresh root.

Jane Fowle's curry powder has a distinctive aroma and taste. Try using the ready-powdered spices in differing proportions before you undertake the labour of drying and grinding your own.

Blend all the ingredients, using only a pinch of Cayenne at first: you can add more when you find a strength of flavour which pleases you. This mixture is sweeter than most modern curry powders.

Store the mixture in an airtight spice jar or pot. Note that the rice flour in particular does not have a very long shelf life. Use the powder as directed in A Receipt to Curry after the Indian Manner (page 56).

Jemeca 'Trouts'

Take ye herrings take out ye Gutss & take out ye rows & scale y^m lay y^m 1 laying on another salted in a pan 24 hours then take y^m out & wipe y^m dry then put y^m in a pan fit to bake y^m in lay a laying of fish & little Gemeca pepper hool between each laying then fill up the pot wth ye best wine vinagar then bake it 6 howers when it is coold take off ye fat they are then fit to eat & w^ll keep good in their pickle a quarter of year you may eat them wth Oyl Vineger lemmon or pepper. Tie a shet of brown pape over ye pan when it goes into ye Oven. From Hanah Fream.
(D.R. 1698, fac. 1968, page 33.)

MAKES 12 (MINIMUM)

12 small herring (or more) of about the same size, gutted and scaled

salt

20–30 allspice berries (for 12 herrings)

white wine vinegar

garnish of salad leaves and hard-boiled egg yolks (optional)

This recipe for soused herring is perfectly practical today, and makes a good party 'starter' in summer. Note, though, that it is not worth pickling fewer than 12 herrings, nor is it effective. Also, they should be used within 10–12 days of being prepared in spite of the recipe's extravagant claims.

Ask the fishmonger to gut and scale the herrings. Take off the heads. Rinse the fish in cold water. Wipe dry with kitchen paper (paper towels).

Lay a row of herrings side by side in a square or oblong non-metallic baking-dish. Sprinkle well with salt. Repeat the layers until you have packed in all the fish. Cover and leave in a cool place for 24 hours.

Wipe the surface salt off the fish with kitchen paper and lay the fish on another sheet of paper to dry off slightly. Drain and dry the dish. Then replace the fish, sprinkling each layer with whole allspice berries. Fill the dish with vinegar, cover tightly with foil and leave in the oven overnight at low heat – not more than 275°F/140°C/Gas Mark 1. Next day uncover, skim off any fat floating on the surface of the vinegar, replace the foil and refrigerate until needed.

The best way to serve the 'trouts' is to lay them on shredded lettuce or watercress salad garnished with halved hard-boiled egg yolks.

Gooseberry Vinegar

Bruise gooseberries full ripe in a Mortar, then measure them & to every quart of gooseberries put three quarts of water first boiled, & let it stand to be cold then put the water to the gooseberries & let it stand 24 hours, then strain it through canvas & then flannel & to every gallon of this liquor put one pound of feeding brown sugar, stir it well together and barrel it up. At three quarters of a year it will be fit for use but if it stands longer it is better. This Vinegar is likewise good for Pickles. never stop down your Barrel (M.L., page 30.)

Compiler's note: Fruit vinegars like Martha's make a delicious change from the standard ones we all use, and a glut of garden gooseberries may be well employed by country-dwellers for use in sharp salad dressings.

Fruit Butters and Cheeses

From the sixteenth century, apples, pears and soft fruits improved so much in quality that cooked fruit mixtures became very popular for pies and tarts and as spreads. Dark-coloured mulberries, currants and black-berries in particular supplemented well the less tasty but pectin-rich apples for making the stiff mixtures which came to be called jams and, because they were the same consistency as the dairy foods, butters and cheeses. Although adults enjoyed them and served them to guests, they were also considered wholesome (and cheap) treats for children.

In one of Jane's letters we find references to 'black butter' (perhaps blackberry and apple) being eaten by her family as a treat. We do not have a printed source for that recipe, but we do have one written only twelve years after Jane died for a children's dish. It comes from Meg Dods's cookbook, originally published in 1829, and is given below.

Black Butter
(For Children, a Cheap Preserve)
Pick currants, gooseberries, strawberries, or whatever fruit you have: to every two
pounds of fruit put one of sugar, and boil till a good deal reduced.
(M.D. 1829 edn, fac. 1988, page 435.)

redcurrants

blackcurrants

gooseberries

strawberries

apples

sugar

For a modern recipe a mixture of some or all of the above fruits can be used. For each 2 lb/1 kg fruit, allow 1 lb/450 g white sugar. De-stalk and rinse the fruits, making sure that none is mouldy. Mix them and heat gently in a pan until the juices start to run. Stir in the sugar until dissolved, and boil until very thick. Pour into small, hot jars and cover as for jam.

This is a lovely old country preserve, almost unaltered, but shaped by the wise hand of Mary Norwak. She says it is ideal for using up the odd bits and pieces in the freezer.

Lemon Mincemeat

Take a good Lemon, squeese out the Juice, boil the Pulp with the rind tender, &
pound it very fine; put to it three quarters of a pound of currants, half a pd. of
Sugar, half an oz: of Orange flour water a good glass of Mountain or Brandy put
in your juice with half a Nutmeg a little Mace Cittron or candied Orange peel as
you please. You must put three quarters of a pd. of Beef Suet Chopt very fine &
mixed with the Currants. [Added by another hand:] Half a doz. Apples chopt fine
& added to it, is a great improvement. (M.L. page 33.)

MAKES 4 LB/1.8 KG

1 large lemon

12 oz/350 g/2 ½ cups currants

6 oz/175 g/1 cup chopped hard green apple

8 oz/225 g/1 ¼ cups white sugar

4 oz/110 g/⅔ cup cut mixed peel

6 oz/175 g/1 ½ cups shredded beef suet

½ teaspoon grated nutmeg

½ teaspoon ground cinnamon

¼ teaspoon ground mace

¼ teaspoon salt

a little freshly ground black pepper

1 tablespoon orange-flower water

3 fl oz/75 ml/5 tablespoons Malaga wine or brandy

Squeeze the lemon and strain the juice. Boil the pulp and rind until soft,
then process to a paste in an electric blender. In a large bowl, mix all the
dry ingredients thoroughly, then mix in the lemon paste, and lastly all the
liquids including the lemon juice. If the mincemeat is to be kept for any
length of time, cook in the oven for 1 hour at 225–250°F/110–130°C/Gas
Mark ¼–½. Fill into 2 × 2 lb/1 kg jars and label.

Use to fill large or small shortcrust pastry mince pie cases (shells) as you
prefer.

Marmalett of Aprecoks

Take a pounde of aprecoks before they be too ripe; whilst they be very paile, pare them, and stone them, and cutt them in foure peeces, or smaler, as you please; then put in a pounde and a quarter of fine sugar beaten fine, then strayne in a quarter of a pinte of the juce of white courents; or pipin water, set it over the fire, and when the suger is melted, boyle it very fast, and keepe it stiring and scimed till it be cleere and jelly. (R.P. 1974, page 213.)

MAKES 2 LB/1 KG

12 oz/350 g dried apricots

10 fl oz/275 ml/1 ¼ cups apple-water (see method)

1 ¼ lb/550 g/3 cups preserving sugar

Made before 1740, Rebecca Price's 'marmalett' might be either a fruit paste or a whole-fruit jellied conserve made with 'apple-water' (and sometimes called a jelly). Preserves like these, including jams, stayed largely unchanged until the nineteenth century.

Cut up the dried apricots and soak in water for several hours or overnight. While soaking them, make apple-water as follows: wash, peel and core windfalls or cooking apples, and put the peelings and cores into a large saucepan. They should be just covered when you add 1 pint/575 ml/2 ½ cups water. Simmer them, covered, until they are very soft and the water is well flavoured. Measure the water to make sure that you have well over 10 fl oz/275 ml/1 ¼ cups apple-water.

Drain the apricots and put them in a large saucepan or a preserving pan with the sugar. Add the apple-water and bring slowly to the boil, skimming occasionally. Cook steadily until the syrup sheets a spoon and drips from it slowly in blobs, then skim again and test for setting quality by dropping a few drips on to a cold plate. They should 'jelly' on contact with the plate.

Pour the 'marmalett' into hot jars: to avoid making air bubbles, pour it in down the side of the jar. Take out any air bubbles which *do* form by prodding with a skewer. Cover the preserve with waxed paper circles and leave to cool. As soon as it is cold, cover the jar or jars, and label them with the name of the preserve and the date on which it was made. Do not rely on your memory. Store the 'marmalett' in a cool, dry place.

Orange Peel 'Straws' in Syrup

Mrs Rundell (M.R. 1806 edn, page 196.) suggested 'small strips of orange-paring cut thin' as an alternative to candied peel 'chips' for decorating desserts. Slivers of peel by themselves soon dry out. But you can use the following short-cut way of making a decorative syrupy topping for desserts which keeps for ages. The idea of layering sugar and peel comes from John Farley's recipe for candying angelica.

Sterilise by boiling a jam-pot or mustard-pot with a flat-topped screw-on lid. Pare the thin coloured peel from one or more oranges with a potato peeler. Cut the peel into 'matchstick' strips and blanch them for 30 seconds–1 minute in boiling water. Drain. Then pack alternate layers of peel and granulated (coarse) sugar into your pot, ending with sugar. While filling, tap the pot on the worktop occasionally to knock out air pockets. Screw the lid on tightly. Then, every day for a fortnight, turn the pot upside down (or the right way up).

The shredded peel can then be stored in the same pot for use. Note, however, that it will pack down, leaving space for 'topping up' with more peel and sugar when convenient.

The peel will keep for a long time. It is delicious as a topping for ice-cream or, in winter, for fruit salads. It is even more pleasant if mixed with a pinch of dried mixed herbs or spice.

Raspberry 'Vinegar' (Cordial)

*Put two quarts of large fine Rasberries into one quart of the best Vinegar, let it
stand 10 days near a fire, clarify a pd. of fine Sugar, strain off the juice from the
Rasberries, add the clarified Syrop & boil all together till it is fine – When it is
cold put it into small Bottles & use it as you would Orgeat, mix it with Water to
your taste – Mrs. Lefroy. (M.L., page 67.)*

Makes about 3 pints/1.7 litres/7½ cups

3 lb/1.4 kg fresh or defrosted frozen raspberries

3 pints/1.7 litres/7½ cups distilled white vinegar

white sugar

Put the raspberries and vinegar in a bowl and leave, covered, for 5–6
days, stirring occasionally. Mash well and strain through a jelly bag
without exerting any pressure. Measure the liquid and allow 1 lb/450 g
sugar to each 1 pint/575 ml liquid. Bring to the boil slowly, stirring well to
dissolve the sugar. Simmer for 20 minutes. Skim and leave until cold.
Pour into sterilized screw-top bottles or jars and seal tightly. Use a
tablespoon of raspberry vinegar in a glass of cold water as a cooling drink
or to soothe a cold or fever. If you want a fuller-flavoured drink use a little
more of the mixture.

This used to be a great treat for country children, but it is more often used
now as a drink for wise drivers. (Orgeat was a similar cooling drink made
from barley or almonds and orange-flower water.)

Mary Norwak's unrivalled knowledge of country lore has supplied this
modern version of the old traditional recipe from her book *The Farmhouse
Kitchen.*

Mrs Fowle's Orange Wine

*Take ten Galn. of Water, 30 lbs of fine Lisbon Sugar & the Whites of 6 Eggs
well beaten, boil it together three quarters of an hour skimming it well & then add
the juice of 33 Seville Oranges (reserving the Peel of 24 of them to throw into the
Barrel) the juice of 36 sweet Oranges & of fifteen Lemons mix all well together &
boil it up again – When cold for working take a large toast cover it with good yeast
& let it work for two days & two nights, then tun it. – Rack it off at the end of
four Months, rinse the Cask & replace the Liquor with a Bottle of Brandy & three
pd. of Lump Sugar. – You may bottle it towards the end of the Year –
Mrs. C. Fowle. (M.L., page 79.)*

MAKES ABOUT 1 GALLON/4.5 LITRES/10 US PINTS

3 good-sized Seville oranges

4 sweet oranges

1 ½ lemons

1 gallon/4.5 litres/10 US pints water

3 lb/1.4 kg/7 cups white sugar

1 oz/25 g compressed fresh yeast

1 slice toast

3 fl oz/75 ml/5 tablespoons brandy

5 oz/150 g lump sugar

Peel the Seville oranges and reserve the peel. Squeeze the juice of all the
oranges and the lemons and put it with the water in a 2-gallon/
9-litre/20-US-pint non-metallic flameproof pan. Bring to the boil, add
the sugar and stir well to dissolve. Leave to cool.

When cold, spread the yeast on a slice of toast and float it on the liquid.
Leave for 48 hours, then remove the yeast-covered toast.

Transfer the liquid to a cask or similar non-metal container. Add the
reserved orange peel, then seal the container with a fermentation lock.
Leave it to 'work' and then mature it, lightly corked and covered with a
cloth, for 4 months.

After 4 months, strain off the liquid and rinse out the cask. Return the
liquid with the brandy and lump sugar. Seal the cask and allow it to stand
for 8 months longer. Then strain and bottle your wine in sterilised
bottles; used warmed, wetted corks and push them in firmly but not too
tightly.

Negus

Negus was 'invented', so it is said, by one Colonel Francis Negus in Queen Anne's time. In fact it was, and is, a form of mulled wine. The only difference is that, whereas mulled wine was properly heated by immersing a red-hot poker in the brew, negus was, shamefully, heated in a saucepan. Despite this, it was an extremely popular party drink throughout Georgian and early Victorian times, and it was certainly a good deal less harmful than many others. This version comes from Mary Norwak's extensive library.

MAKES ABOUT 3 PINTS/1.7 LITRES/7½ CUPS

1 pint/575 ml/2½ cups port wine

1 lemon

12 sugar lumps

2 pints/1.1 litres/5 cups boiling water

grated nutmeg

Pour the port into a large, heatproof jug. Rub the lemon with the sugar lumps, then squeeze the lemon juice and strain it. Mix the sugar and lemon juice with the port, and add the boiling water. Cover the jug until the liquid has cooled a bit, then serve in glasses with a scrap of grated nutmeg.

Spruce Beer

White spruce-beer—*To five gallons of water put seven pounds of loaf-sugar, and three-fourths of a pound of the essence of spruce. Boil and skim this. Put it into a vessel, and, when nearly cool, add fresh yeast (about a half-pint or less.) When the beer has fermented for three days, bung the cask, and in a week bottle it off. N.B.—For* Brown *spruce use treacle or coarse brown sugar, instead of loaf-sugar. (M.D. 1829, fac. 1988, pages 471–2.)*

In spite of much searching, we have been quite unable to trace any essence of spruce at all, let alone 12 oz/350 g. We hope that our readers will make and enjoy Martha's ginger beer instead.

Ginger Beer

fit to drink in 24 hours
Two Gallons of Water, 2 oz. cream of Tartar 2 lb. lump Sugar 2 lemons sliced,
2 oz. Ginger bruised, pour the water boiling on the ingredients, then add 2
spoonfuls of good Yeast; when cold bottle it in stone bottles and tie the corks down.
(M.L., page 97.)

MAKES ABOUT 1 GALLON/4.5 LITRES/10 US PINTS

2 lemons

1¼ lb/550 g/3 cups granulated (coarse) sugar

1 oz/25 g piece fresh ginger root, peeled and bruised

1 teaspoon cream of tartar

1 gallon/4.5 litres/10 US pints boiling water

1 tablespoon compressed fresh yeast

Perhaps we moderns have weak stomachs, but most traditional ginger beer recipes seem distinctly gassy in effect for about 4 days after making. Use bottles with screw-on tops if possible. If you must use corks, tie them on securely.

Remove the yellow outer rinds of the lemons as thinly as possible. Discard all the white pith. Cut the fruit into thin slices, removing the pips. Put the sliced lemon and rind into a non-metallic bowl with the sugar, ginger and cream of tartar. Pour on the boiling water, and leave until it has cooled to blood heat. Cream the yeast with a little of the liquid, then stir it into the mixture. Cover it with a cloth and leave it in a fairly warm place for 24 hours. Skim the yeast off the top, then strain the liquid off the sediment. Bottle and leave for 4 days in a cool place before use. Consume without delay as the beer does not keep long.

This modern version of ginger beer is adapted from one in the 1966 revised reprint of the sixth edition of *Farmhouse Fare*, published by Countrywise Books in 1963.

Assemblies and Suppers

White Soup

To six quarts of water put in a knuckle of veal, a large fowl, and a pound of lean bacon, and half a pound of rice, with two anchovies, a few pepper corns, two or three onions, a bundle of sweet herbs, three or four heads of celery in slices, stew all together, till your soup is as strong as you choose it, then strain it through a hair sieve into a clean earthen pot, let it stand all night, then take off the scum, and pour it clear off into a tossing-pan, put in half a pound of Jordan almonds beat fine, boil it a little and run it through a lawn sieve, then put in a pint of cream and the yolk of an egg.—Make it hot, and send it to the table.
(E.R. 1782, fac. 1970, page 12.)

SERVES 6 GENEROUSLY

6 pints/3.4 litres/15 cups water

1 medium-sized boiling fowl or chicken

8 oz/225 g lean bacon or gammon trimmings

4 oz/110 g/½ cup white rice

6 black peppercorns

2 onions, peeled and halved

2 canned anchovy fillets

2–3 sprigs each thyme, marjoram and tarragon (or other sweet herbs), tied in a cloth

4–6 stalks celery, chopped

4 oz/110 g/1 cup ground almonds

1 egg yolk

10 fl oz/275 ml/1¼ cups single (light) cream

whipped cream and watercress leaves to garnish (optional)

Mrs Raffald called her White Soup 'excellent', and compared with other versions I have found it good without being pretentious.

Pour the water into a large stew-pan. Rinse the chicken inside, then add it to the pan with any giblets (you can joint it first if you like). Add the bacon, rice, peppercorns, onions, anchovies, herbs and celery. Cover the pan, bring to the boil and cook very gently until the chicken meat is fully cooked and the liquid is flavoursome.

Strain the stock into a bowl, cover it with a cloth and leave in a cold place for several hours or overnight. Next day, skim off any fat and impurities and pour the stock into a clean pan. Add the ground almonds, bring slowly to the boil and simmer for 10 minutes. Strain it yet again, this time through cheesecloth. Whisk the egg yolk into the single cream and add to the soup, which should be slightly cooled by the straining. Reheat until very hot, but on no account let the soup boil again. You can 'improve' the soup by serving it with a teaspoon of whipped cream or a few watercress leaves on each bowlful.

Asparagus Dressed the Italian Way

Take the asparagus, break them in pieces, then boil them soft and drain the water from them; take a little oil, water, and vinegar, let it boil, season it with pepper and salt, throw in the asparagus and thicken with yolks of eggs ... the Spaniards add sugar, but that spoils them. (H.G. 1796, fac. 1971, page 233.)

SERVES 6

about 60 stems fresh asparagus

salt and pepper

3 tablespoons white wine vinegar

3 egg yolks

about 5 oz/150 g/⅔ cup butter, flaked

Cut any woody ends off the asparagus stems and scrape the white parts if needed. Tie the stems in bundles with all the heads at one end and trim the stem ends level. Put a pan of lightly salted water on the stove and stand the bundles upright in the pan so that the stems are almost covered; only the heads should be above water level. Simmer for 10–15 minutes. Then lay the bundles flat in the pan and simmer for another 5–10 minutes until the heads are tender. Drain thoroughly. (Small, thin asparagus or sprue cooks in 5 minutes.)

When they are ready, cut the tender green heads and stems of the asparagus into 1-inch/2.5-cm pieces, and keep warm in a serving dish.

In a small pan, boil the vinegar and 1½ tablespoons water until reduced to about 3 tablespoons. Cool slightly. Beat the egg yolks until liquid in a heatproof bowl, then stir in the vinegar. Place the bowl over simmering water and stir until the mixture thickens. Gradually whisk in as much of the butter as the egg sauce will hold without separating, sprinkling in a little salt and pepper as you do so. The sauce should be thick and quite sharp to the palate. Serve it over the asparagus while still warm.

Buttered Prawns

Take about two quarts, and pick out their tails. Bruise the bodies, and put them into about a pint of white wine, with a blade of mace. Let them stew a quarter of an hour, then stir them together, and strain them. Then wash out the saucepan, and put to it the strained liquor and tails. Grate into it a small nutmeg, add a little salt, and a quarter of a pound of butter rolled in flour. Shake it all together; cut a pretty thin toast round a quartern loaf, toast it brown on both sides, cut it into six pieces, lay it close together in the bottom of your dish, and pour your fish and sauce over it. Send it hot to table. If it be craw-fish or prawns, garnish your dish with some of the biggest claws laid thick round. Water will do instead of wine, by only adding a spoonful of vinegar. (J.F. 7th edn, page 86.)

SERVES 4

1 lb/450 g fresh or frozen cooked prawns with heads and shells on

5 fl oz/150 ml/scant ⅔ cup dry white wine

1 piece of blade mace or good pinch of grated nutmeg

1 slice bread, ½ inch/1 cm thick, cut horizontally through a round loaf

butter for spreading

small pinch of salt

a few grains of Cayenne pepper

2 oz/50 g/4 tablespoons softened butter blended with 2 tablespoons flour

chopped fresh parsley

If using frozen prawns, thaw them. Behead and shell the prawns whether frozen or fresh. Put the heads and shells in a pan with the wine and 5 fl oz/150 ml/scant ⅔ cup water. Add the spice and simmer until the liquid is reduced to 6 fl oz/175 ml/⅔ cup. Strain it into a clean pan.

Toast the bread on both sides and butter one side. Cut into 4 or 6 wedges and keep warm.

Add the salt, Cayenne and butter-flour mixture to the liquid in the pan and place it over low heat. Cook gently, stirring continuously, until the butter melts and the sauce thickens. Add the prawns and cook for 2–3 minutes to heat them through.

Serve the prawns and sauce on the toast, buttered side up, as an eighteenth-century corner dish at dinner or as a modern supper dish. Sprinkle with parsley before serving.

Note: 1 pint/575 ml/2½ cups British prawns in the shell weigh 10 oz/275 g.

Petit Pasties

Make a short crust, roll it thick, make them about as big as the bowl of a spoon and about an inch deep; take a piece of veal enough to fill the patty, as much bacon and beef-suet, shred them all very fine, season them with pepper and salt, and a little sweet herbs; put them into a little stew-pan, keep turning them about, with a few mushrooms chopped small, for eight or ten minutes; then fill your petty-patties and cover them with some crust; colour them with the yolk of an egg, and bake them. (H.G. 1796, fac. 1971, page 144.)

MAKES 8–10

7 oz/200 g shortcrust pastry

egg wash for glazing

5 oz/150 g lean cooked veal or chicken without gristle or bone

5 oz/150 g rindless bacon rashers (slices), blanched

1 tablespoon shredded suet

salt and pepper to taste

finely grated rind of ½ lemon

1 teaspoon finely chopped fresh parsley

1 oz/25 g mushrooms, finely chopped

about 3 tablespoons white wine sauce (see method)

Make the patty cases first. Pre-heat the oven to 350°F/180°C/Gas Mark 4. Roll out the pastry ⅛ inch/3 mm thick and use two-thirds of it to line small bun tins (muffin pans). Cut the remaining pastry into rounds for lids. Glaze the lids with the egg wash. Place both cases and lids on baking parchment laid on a baking-sheet. Bake 'blind' until firm and golden. Keep aside.

To prepare the filling, mince the veal or chicken and bacon together. Mix with all the other ingredients in a small saucepan. Heat until the mushrooms soften and the sauce is very hot. Fill the mixture into the baked cases, put on the lids and serve at once.

For the white wine sauce, use the sauce mixture suggested for A Pretty Dish of Eggs (see page 93), but without the chopped shallots.

For a party or picnic, bake the cases and lids ahead of time and set them ready for filling. Cook the filling mixture as well, but do not fill the cases until it has cooled thoroughly.

Chickens with Tongues
(A good Dish for a great deal of Company)

Take six small chickens, boiled very white, six hogs tongues boiled and peeled, a cauliflower boiled very white in milk and water whole, and a good deal of spinach boiled green; then lay your cauliflower in the middle, the chickens close all round, and the tongues round them with the roots outward, and the spinach in little heaps between the tongues. Garnish with little pieces of bacon toasted, and lay a little piece on each of the tongues. (H.G. 1796, fac. 1971, pages 104 and 29.)

SERVES 6

6 poussins, boiled or steamed (see method)

1 lemon, cut in half

6 sheeps' or pigs' tongues, boiled and skinned, or boiling sausages
(see method)

1 medium-sized cauliflower, prepared and cooked whole in water (see
method) or 6 oz/175 g/about 1 cup long-grain white rice,
boiled and drained

salt

2 lb/1 kg spinach leaves

12 rashers (slices) middle cut or streaky bacon

This dish illustrates beautifully the Regency delight in symmetry and display, shown in precise shapes and colours – even on the dinner-table. An interesting dish for a small, formal supper.

Mrs Glasse suggests soaking the prepared chickens in milk and water for 2 hours, then rubbing the breasts with lemon juice and dredging them (with flour) before cooking them in the soaking liquid. Using modern birds, you can omit the preliminary soaking and the dredging with flour which only thickens the cooking liquid slightly. Simply rub the breasts of the poussins with the cut side of half a lemon. Then pack them into one or two stew-pans, add enough water to cover their backs, put on the lid(s) and simmer them for about 30 minutes. Alternatively place them on a trivet or upturned plate and steam them; allow about 40 minutes.

Sheeps' tongues weigh about 4 oz/110 g each before cooking and pigs' tongues about 8 oz/225 g. Considering their size, they are a trial to cook, needing 2 hours' simmering or longer. This is fine if you have a farm-house Aga but not otherwise, and I suggest, with due deference to Mrs Glasse, that boiling sausages will provide a suitable flavour contrast to the chickens in an acceptable shape. Boil them as your supplier recommends. (Mrs Glasse herself gives recipes for boiling Bologna and Hamburg sausages.)

Obviously for this green-and-white dish you need a sparklingly white, whole cauliflower. Take off all the surrounding green leaves and cut off the stalk close to the florets so that the head stands upright evenly. Make a cross-cut in the cut base of the stalk, then put the whole head, stalk side down, in a pan which just holds it. Add about 3 inches/7.5 cm slightly salted water to the pan, put a lid on it and cook over medium heat for 25–35 minutes. Check the water level once or twice while cooking. Then check whether the cauliflower is ready by plunging a skewer through it, down into the stalk.

While the cauliflower is cooking, dress the spinach. Rinse it well, put it in a pan which will just hold it and add a scrap of salt, but no water. Cover it closely, set it over medium heat and let it cook, shaking it often, until the leaves are shrunk and the liquid from it bubbles. Drain it well and squeeze it between two plates as Mrs Glasse suggests before you serve it.

Lastly deal with the bacon rashers. If you wish, you can roll them up, then grill (broil) or bake them, turning them over and over. Skewer a bacon roll between the legs or wings of each poussin and on top of each sausage (if using them). Alternatively dice the bacon before cooking it, then scatter it over the finished dish like confetti.

As far as assembling this dish is concerned I cannot better Mrs Glasse's own description at the head of this recipe. If you do not care to subject your guests to the scent of cauliflower, pile boiled long-grain white rice in the centre of your dish instead.

Ice-cream

Pare, stone and scald twelve ripe apricots, beat them fine in a marble mortar, put to them six ounces of double refined sugar, a pint of scalding cream, work it through a hair sieve, put it into a tin that has a close cover, set it in a tub of ice broken small, and a large quantity of salt put amongst it, when you see your cream grow thick round the edges of your tin, stir it, and set it in again till it grows quite thick, when your cream is all froze up, take it out of your tin, and put it into the mould you intend it to be turned out of, then put on the lid, and have ready another tub with ice and salt in as before, put your mould in the middle, and lay your ice under and over it, let it stand four or five hours, dip your tin in warm water when you turn it out; if it be summer, you must not turn it out till the moment you want it: you may use any sort of fruit if you have not apricots, only observe to work it fine.
(E.R. 1792, fac. 1970, page 249.)

SERVES 6

1 lb/450 g large juicy apricots or yellow plums

about 4 oz/110 g/ ⅔ cup caster (superfine) sugar

3 egg yolks, beaten

10 fl oz/275 ml/1 ¼ cups single (light) cream

10 fl oz/275 ml/1 ¼ cups whipping cream

a few drops lemon juice for bland fruit

Set your freezer or refrigerator ice compartment to 'fast freeze'. Wash the fruit, cut it up, then cook it gently until tender with 3 tablespoons water. Sieve it into a clean pan and add as much sugar as the fruit's flavour needs. Do not under-sweeten: freezing dulls flavour. Add the egg yolks and stir them into the pulp, then heat below the boil until the mixture thickens. Taste and add a little more sugar if required.

While the mixture cools, beat the two creams together until thickening, then fold them into the purée. Turn into a lightly oiled, chilled mould. Freeze the ice-cream for 1–2 hours, or until mushy. Beat it briskly, to break down the ice crystals, then refreeze it until you need it. (For really smooth ice-cream, beat and refreeze it a second time before finishing it off.)

As soon as the ice-cream is frozen to the consistency you want, return the freezer or refrigerator half-way back to its normal setting until you are ready to unmould your dessert. Unmould the ice-cream just before serving.

Mr Darcy's chef would have set this ice-cream in a decorative jelly mould, or might have made it like a charlotte in a soufflé dish, surrounded by Naples Biskets (see page 87). It can equally well be served in sundae glasses decorated with crystallized or candied fruits – but not glacé (candied) cherries.

Greengages, white peaches or nectarines, apples or soft fruits can be used instead of apricots or plums.

A Trifle

Take three Naple Biscuits cut them in Slices dip them in sack lay them in the bottom of your dish, then make a custard of a pint of cream & five Eggs & put over them then make a whipt Syllabub as light as possible to cover the whole the higher it is piled the handsomer it looks. (M.L., page 35.)

SERVES 6

1 quantity Solid Custard (see page 61)

plain Madeira cake, cut in 1-inch/2.5-cm slices, to line the bottom and ⅓ of the sides of a 2½-pint/1.4-litre/6¼-cup glass bowl

medium-dry sherry to moisten

1 quantity Solid Syllabub (see page 85)

chopped, candied or crystallized fruits to decorate (optional)

The original Naples biscuits were twice-baked, hard sponge cakes stored for use when needed for eating with or in eighteenth-century sweet 'creams'; I have used instead plain Madeira cake. The sack (sherry) was intended to soften the biscuits, so go easy when adding it to the softer modern cake.

Make the Solid Custard first so that it is cooled (but not set) when you are ready to add it to the sponge cake and before you want to add the syllabub. The dessert will then have interesting, contrasting layers. Follow the original recipe above for adding the syllabub. Use chopped, candied or crystallized fruits, if you wish, for a period-style decoration on top of the trifle.

Little Iced Cakes

Take a p^d of fine flour, a p^d of loaf-sug^r beaten & sifted, and of butter washed in a little rose-water ... together. Stroak in ye butter into ye flour and[?] ye sug^r w^{the} a little mace finely ground [?] and mix all together. take 6 eggs leaving out 2 whites. Beat 'Em and rose-watter into the [?] rest, mixing it wth y^r hand for near a q^r of an Hour ... put in 3 q^{rs} of a p^d of Currants clean wash'd & made dry & put it into pans or little paper-hoops and sift fine sug^r over 'Em, & bak: 'Em in an oven as hot as for manchet. you may make some of 'Em plain ye same way; only putting in cittron or orange instead of Currants: you may ice 'Em wth ye same icing y^t you made for ye great cake.

CAKE ICING

For a large [cake], beat and sift eight ounces of fine sugar, put into a mortar with four spoonfuls of rose-water, with the whites of two eggs beaten and strained, whisk it well, and when the cake is almost cold, dip a feather in the icing, and cover the cake well; set it in the oven to harden, but don't let it stay to discolour. Put the cake in a dry place. (M.R. 1806 edn, page 233.)

MAKES 36–40

8 oz/225 g/1 cup softened butter

1 tablespoon rose-water

1–2 drops rose flavouring (optional)

¼ teaspoon ground mace

8 oz/225 g/1¼ cups caster (superfine) sugar

2 whole eggs and 1 yolk

a few drops lemon or orange juice

14 oz/400 g/3½ cups flour, sifted

Icing

2 oz/50 g/½ cup sifted icing (confectioner's) sugar

1 tablespoon rose-water

rose flavouring (optional)

1 egg white, beaten until liquid

Set the oven to heat to 350°F/180°C/Gas Mark 4. In a fair-sized bowl, beat the softened butter with the rose-water and, if you wish, the rose flavouring for extra taste. Sift in the mace and sugar and beat until they are blended in well. Whisk the eggs and yolk together until frothing, add the juice, then beat them into the butter-sugar mixture in 3 parts, alternately with the sifted flour. Go on beating until blended well.

Put small dollops of dough into buttered bun or tartlet tins (patty tins) 2 inches/5 cm across and ½ inch/1 cm deep. Bake for 10–12 minutes (no more), then cool on a wire rack.

When they have cooled, place the cakes side by side on a baking-sheet. Blend together the icing ingredients. With a pastry brush, cover the tops of the cakes with icing. Put them in the oven heated again to 350°F/180°C/Gas Mark 4 for 2–3 minutes, until the icing has hardened. Serve cold.

Some eighteenth-century cakes were brushed with icing before baking, but this dough softens and spreads too much. Earlier cake icings were stiffened with gum tragacanth, a plant product, but according to the writer Alice Prochaska it was not needed after powdered icing sugar came into use.

The recipe for these little cakes was very kindly supplied by antiques collector and dealer Joanna Booth.

Martha's Almond Cheesecakes

Take half a pd. of blanch'd almonds pounded small with a spoonful of Orange flower water & half a pound of double-refined sugar 10 yolks of Eggs well beat add the peels of two oranges or Lemons which must be boil'd very tender then beat in a Mortar very fine, then mix them altogether & put in three quarters of a pound of melted butter being almost cold & bake it in good Crust. (M.L., pages 32–3.)

MAKES 24–28

1 large lemon or orange

4 oz/110 g/⅔ cup caster (superfine) sugar, plus
1 extra tablespoon for sprinkling

a few drops orange-flower water

4 oz/110 g/1 cup ground almonds

2 whole eggs, separated, plus 2 egg whites

2 oz/50 g/4 tablespoons butter, melted and cooled

1 lb/450 g shortcrust pastry

Pare the rind of the lemon or orange thinly, taking off the top coloured layer only. Boil the parings in a small pan of water until soft; drain. Pulverize them with some of the sugar in an electric blender or grinder. Put them in a bowl, add the rest of the sugar and the orange-flower water, then mix in the ground almonds.

Beat the whole eggs until liquid and combine them with the almond mixture and the cooled, melted butter. Whisk the 2 egg whites until semi-stiff and fold them into the mixture; the texture should be that of a coating custard. Chill the mixture if you have not yet made the pastry cases.

Set the oven to heat to 375°F/190°C/Gas Mark 5. Roll out the pastry to ⅛ inch/3 mm thickness, 'rest' it, and cut it into rounds to fit tartlet tins (patty pans) about 2½ inches/6.5 cm across and ¾ inch/2 cm deep. Line the tins with pastry, pricking the bottom of each and sprinkling it with a little sugar. Fill three-quarters full with the almond mixture, then bake for 20 minutes. Cool on a wire rack.

You can ice these tartlets if you like, as for the cakes on page 122.

Rout Drop Cakes

Mix two pounds of flour, one ditto butter, one ditto sugar, one ditto currants, clean and dry; then wet into a stiff paste, with 2 eggs, a large spoonful of orange-flower water, ditto rose-water, ditto sweet wine, ditto brandy, drop on a tin-plate floured: a very short time bakes them. (M.R. 1806 edn, page 235.)

MAKES 16–20

5 oz/150 g/1¼ cups plain (all-purpose) flour

pinch of salt

2 oz/50 g/4 tablespoons softened butter

2 oz/50 g/⅓ cup caster (superfine) sugar

1 small egg

½ teaspoon orange juice

½ teaspoon rose-water

1 teaspoon sweet white wine or sherry

1 teaspoon brandy

1 oz/25 g/¼ cup currants

Set the oven to heat to 350°F/180°C/Gas Mark 4. Sift the flour and salt into a bowl. Work in the butter to make a crumbly mixture, then add the sugar. In a small bowl, beat the egg until liquid. Add the juice, rose-water, wine or sherry, and brandy. Stir well. Then mix the liquids by degrees into the dry goods, to obtain a smooth dough. Lastly mix in the fruit.

Put the cake mixture in small, neat heaps (¾ inch/2 cm across) on a lightly greased baking-sheet. Bake in the oven for 16–18 minutes. Cool on a wire rack.

These little cakes are pleasant with a glass of wine or cup of coffee at mid-morning or in the evening. They were easy-to-eat party cookies on a Georgian evening tea-table too.

Ratafia Cakes

Take 8 oz: of apricot kernels, if they cannot be had bitter Almonds will do as well, blanch them & beat them very fine with a little Orrange flower water, mix them with the whites of three eggs well beaten & put to them two pounds of single refin'd Sugar finely beaten & sifted, work all together and it will be like a paste, then lay it in little round bits on tin plates flour'd, set them in an oven that is not very hot & they will puff up & be soon be baked [sic]. (M.L., page 47.)

MAKES 36–40

4 oz/110 g/1 cup ground almonds

2 egg whites

1 teaspoon orange-flower water or orange liqueur

6 oz/175 g/¾ cup caster (superfine) sugar

rice paper

Today we know that bitter almonds may contain prussic acid, so it is wise to use ready-ground sweet almonds and a little orange liqueur for extra flavour instead.

Set the oven to heat to 350°F/180°C/Gas Mark 4. Sieve or pound the almonds in a bowl to get rid of any lumps. In a second bowl, whisk the egg whites with the orange-flower water or liqueur until stiff. Then mix the sugar into the almonds thoroughly and lastly fold in the whisked whites.

Cover a baking-sheet with rice paper and place small teaspoonfuls of mixture on it, well spaced apart. Bake for 10–12 minutes or until the cakes are just fawn; they must still be soft underneath. Cool them on the sheet, then keep in an airtight tin. Enjoy them with after-dinner coffee.

Mr Darcy's Dinner or the
Dinner Which Never Happened

A MENU OF 2 COURSES AND A DESSERT COURSE OR TEA-BOARD SUITABLE FOR A COUNTRY GENTLEMAN AND 10–12 GUESTS IN SUMMER. THERE ARE 9 DISHES IN EACH COURSE

First Course

Centre dishes: White Soup removed for Plaice; Dressed Lamb, Garnished; Chickens with Tongues; Fricassee of Turnips.
Side and corner dishes: Buttered Prawns; Asparagus Dressed the Italian Way; Macaroni; Sole with Wine and Mushrooms; Broccoli served hot.

Second Course

Centre dishes: Pheasant à la Braise; Ragoo of Celery with Wine; Forcemeat Balls; Wine-roasted Gammon [served cold].
Side and corner dishes: Apple Pie; Marmalett of Aprecoks; Jaune Mange; Trifle; Ice-cream.

Dessert

Almonds; Raisins; Preserves.

Tea Board

Tea; Negus; Raspberry Cordial; Apple Puffs; Fine Cake; Little Iced Cakes; Ratafia Cakes; Naples Biskets.

Further Reading

Addams, Samuel and Sarah. *The Complete Servant*, Lewes, 1989.

Austen, Jane. *Sense and Sensibility*, ed. R. W. Chapman, Oxford, 3rd edn, rep. 1967.

Pride and Prejudice, ed. R. W. Chapman, Oxford, 3rd edn, rep. 1967.

Mansfield Park, ed. R. W. Chapman, Oxford, 3rd edn, rep. 1966.

Emma, ed. R. W. Chapman, Oxford, 3rd edn, rep. 1966.

Northanger Abbey and *Persuasion*, ed. R. W. Chapman, Oxford, 3rd edn, rep. 1965.

Minor Works, ed. R. W. Chapman, Oxford, rev. edn, 1963.

Catharine and Other Writings, ed. M. A. Doody and D. Murray, Oxford, 1993.

Jane Austen's Letters, ed. Deirdre Le Faye, Oxford, 3rd edn, 1995.

Austen-Leigh, James Edward. *A Memoir of Jane Austen*, ed. R. W. Chapman, Oxford, 1926, rep. 1951.

Beresford, John, ed. *The Diary of a Country Parson, 1758–1802* [Revd James Woodforde], Oxford, 1935, rep. 1963.

Black, Maggie, with Brears, P., and others. *A Taste of History: 10,000 Years of Food in Britain*, London, 1993.

Brennan, Flora, trans. and ed. *Pückler's Progress: the Adventures of Prince Pückler-Muskau in England, Wales and Ireland as told in letters to his former wife, 1826–29*, London, 1987.

Brown, Peter. *Pyramids of Pleasure; Eating and Dining in 18th Century England*, Civic Trust, York, 1990.

The Keeping of Christmas: England's Festive Tradition 1760–1840, Civic Trust, York, 1992.

Burnett, John. *Plenty & Want: a social history of diet in England from 1815 to the present day*, London 1979.

Burton, Elizabeth. *The Georgians at Home*, London, 1967.

Cecil, Lord David. *A Portrait of Jane Austen*, London, 1978.

Davies, Jennifer. *The Victorian Kitchen Garden*, London, 1987.

The Victorian Kitchen, London, 1989.

Eales, Mrs Mary. *Receipts* (1718); later known as *The Compleat Confectioner* (1733), fac. rep. of 1733 edn, London, 1985.

Emmerson, Robin. *Table Settings*, Princes Risborough, 1991.

Eveleigh, David J. *Firegrates and Kitchen Ranges*, Princes Risborough, 1983.

Old Cooking Utensils, Princes Risborough, 1986.

Fearn, Jacqueline. *Domestic Bygones*, Princes Risborough, 1977.

Frazer, Mrs. *The Practice of Cookery, &c.*, Edinburgh, 3rd edn, 1800.

Harrison, Molly. *The Kitchen in History*, Reading, 1972.

Hartley, Dorothy. *Food in England*, London, 1954, rep. 1979.

Le Faye, Deirdre, and Austen-Leigh, W. and R. A. *Jane Austen: A Family Record*, London, 1989, rep. 1993.

Mitford, Mary Russell. *Our Village*, 5 vols, London, 1824–32; many modern selections and reprints.

Lady Montagu of Beaulieu. *To the Manor Born*, London, 1971.

Palmer, Arnold. *Movable Feasts: changes in English eating-habits*, ed. and intro. David Pocock, Oxford, 1984.

Prochaska, Alice and Frank, eds. *Margaretta Acworth's Georgian Cookery Book*, London, 1987.

Quayle, Eric. *Old Cook Books: an Illustrated History*, London, 1978.

Simond, Louis. *An American in Regency England, the journal of a tour in 1810–1811*, ed. and intro. Christopher Hibbert, London, 1968.

Smith, Mrs. *The Compleat Housewife, or, Accomplish'd Gentlewoman's Companion*, fac. rep. of 15th edn 1753, London, 1968 and 1973.

Smith, W. H. Ltd. *Town & Country Kitchens, Everyday Collectables*, London, 1991.

Stuart, David. *The Kitchen Garden: A Historical Guide to Traditional Crops*, London, 1984, rep. Gloucester 1987.

Tannahill, Reay. *Regency England*, London 1964.

Verral, William. *A Complete System of Cookery*, London, 1759; new edn by Ann Haly, Lewes, 1988.

White, Gilbert. *Journals, 1751–93*, ed. Francesca Greenoak, 3 vols, London, 1986.

Williams, E. N. *Life in Georgian England*, London 1962.

Wilson, C. Anne. *Food and Drink in Britain: from the Stone Age to Recent Times*, London, 1973 and 1976.

SOURCES CITED

C.C.   Charles Carter. *The Complete Practical Cook*, London, 1730, fac. 1984.

D.R.   Dr Dennis Rhodes. *In an Eighteenth Century Kitchen: A Receipt Book of Cookery 1698*, London 1968, reissued 1983.

E.R.   Elizabeth Raffald. *The Experienced English Housekeeper*, London, 1792, fac. 1970.

H.G.   Hannah Glasse. *The Art of Cookery made Plain & Easy*, London, 1796, fac. 1971.

J.F.   John Farley. *The London Art of Cookery*, 7th edn, London, 1792.

L.P.   Mrs Lybbe Powys MS.

M.D.   Meg Dods. *Cook and Housewife's Manual*, 4th edn 1829, fac. Edinburgh, 1988.

M.L.   Martha Lloyd MS.

M.R.   Maria Rundell. *A New System of Domestic Cookery*, London, 1806 edn.

R.B.   Richard Bradley. *The Country Housewife and Lady's Director*, 1727 (Part I) and 1732 (Part II), combined edn 1736, London, fac. 1980.

R.P.   Rebecca Price. MS trs. M. Masson, *The Compleat Cook*, London, 1974.

S.McI.   Susanna MacIver. *Cookery and Pastry*, Edinburgh, 1782.

W.K.   Dr W. Kitchiner. *The Cook's Oracle*, Edinburgh, 1836.

Acknowledgments are due to Oxford University Press for permission to quote from the editions of Jane Austen's works listed above.

Subject Index of Recipes